DEATHLY EXPERIMENTS

AMS Studies in the Renaissance

ISSN 0195-8011

Series ISBN-13: 978-0-404-61460-7

No. 49

Deathly Experiments

A Study of Icons and Emblems
of Mortality
in
Christopher Marlowe's Plays

ISBN-13: 978-0-404-62349-4

DEATHLY EXPERIMENTS

A STUDY OF ICONS AND EMBLEMS OF MORTALITY IN CHRISTOPHER MARLOWE'S PLAYS

CLAYTON G. MACKENZIE

AMS PRESS, INC.
NEW YORK

Library of Congress Cataloging-in-Publication Data

MacKenzie, Clayton G.
Deathly experiments : a study of icons and emblems of mortality in Christopher Marlowe's
plays / Clayton G. MacKenzie.
    p. cm. — (Studies in the Renaissance, ISSN 0195-8011 ; no. 49)
    Includes bibliographical references and index.
    ISBN 978-0-404-62349-4 (cloth : alk. paper)
    1. Marlowe, Christopher, 1564–1593—Criticism and interpretation. 2. Death in
    literature. I. Title.
PR2677.D4M33   2010
822'.3—dc22   2010029311

All AMS books are printed on acid-free paper that meets the guidelines for performance and
durability of the Committee on Production Guidelines for Book Longevity of the Council on
Library Resources.

AMS Press, Inc.
Brooklyn Navy Yard, 63 Flushing Ave.–Unit #221
Brooklyn, New York 11205-1073, USA
www.amspressinc.com

MANUFACTURED IN THE UNITED STATES OF AMERICA

Contents

List of Illustrations

Figure 1: "The Dangers of Love." Guillaume de la Perrière, *Le Theatre des bons engins* (Paris: Denis Janot, 1544), fol. L4^v. Reproduced with the kind permission of the University of Glasgow Library, Department of Special Collections.

Figure 2: "The Emperor." Hans Holbein, *Imagines Mortis* (Lyon: Ioannes et Franciscus Fellonii, fratres, 1545), fol. A6^r. Reproduced with the kind permission of the University of Glasgow Library, Department of Special Collections.

Figure 3: "The Knight." Hans Holbein, *Imagines Mortis* (Lyon: Ioannes et Franciscus Fellonii, fratres, 1545), fol. C2^r. Reproduced with the kind permission of the University of Glasgow Library, Department of Special Collections.

Figure 4: "Desiderans Dissolvi." Georgette de Montenay, *Emblematvm Christianorvm Centvria* (Zurich: 1571), fol. B1^r. Reproduced with the kind permission of the University of Glasgow Library, Department of Special Collections.

Figure 5: "Death is no Losse." George Wither, *A Collection of Emblemes, Ancient and Moderne* (London: 1635), 21. Reproduced with the kind permission of the University of Glasgow Library, Department of Special Collections.

Figure 6: "The Pedlar." Hans Holbein, *Imagines Mortis* (Lyon: Ioannes et Franciscus Fellonii, fratres, 1545), fol. C5^r. Reproduced with the kind permission of the University of Glasgow Library, Department of Special Collections.

Figure 7: "Fortuna." Jan Van der Noot, *A Theatre for Worldlings* (London: Henry Bynneman, 1569), fol. E2^r. Reproduced with the kind permission of the University of Glasgow Library, Department of Special Collections.

Figure 8: "Quæ pondere maior." Henry Peacham, *Minerva Britanna: Or A Garden of Heroycal Devices* (London: William Dight, 1612), 44. Reproduced with the kind permission of the University of Glasgow Library, Department of Special Collections.

Figure 9: "The Abbot." Hans Holbein, *Imagines Mortis* (Lyon: Ioannes et Franciscus Fellonii, fratres, 1545), fol. A9^v. Reproduced with the kind permission of the University of Glasgow Library, Department of Special Collections.

Figure 10: Memorial for Thomas Gooding, Norwich Cathedral, England.

Figure 11: "The Cardinal." Hans Holbein, *Imagines Mortis* (Lyon: Ioannes et Franciscus Fellonii, fratres, 1545), fol. A7^r. Reproduced with the kind permission of the University of Glasgow Library, Department of Special Collections.

Figure 12: "The King." Hans Holbein, *Imagines Mortis* (Lyon: Ioannes et Franciscus Fellonii, fratres, 1545), fol. A6^v. Reproduced with the kind permission of the University of Glasgow Library, Department of Special Collections.

Figure 13: "Voluptas Ærumnosa." Geffrey Whitney, *A Choice of Emblemes* (Leyden: Christopher Plantin, 1586), 15. Reproduced with the kind permission of the University of Glasgow Library, Department of Special Collections.

Figure 14: "The Castle of Knowledge." Robert Record, *The Castle of Knowledge* (London: R. Wolfe, 1556), frontispiece. Reproduced with the kind permission of the University of Glasgow Library, Department of Special Collections.

In memory of
Mel Arthurs and Kevin Arthurs,
gentlemen and scholars

Acknowledgments

I am grateful to the University Grants Committee of Hong Kong for funding the research for this book through a Competitive Earmarked Research grant.

During my work the staff at the following libraries provided me with a warm welcome and untiring support: Hong Kong Baptist University Library in Hong Kong, the British Library in London, the Stirling Maxwell Collection at the University of Glasgow in Scotland, and the J. R. Ritman Library in Amsterdam. I am especially grateful to David Weston, Keeper of Special Collections at the University of Glasgow Library and to Rubem Amaral, Jr. whose knowledge of the emblem books and sheer enthusiasm drove me on at an important stage of my work. Roseleen Arthurs has been an inspiration to all who know her over these last two years, and I am no exception. My thanks to Geralyn and Brian, Siobhan and Eamonn and the Kelly kids for their generous hospitality and companionship. Rebecca and Simon Brown, and little Georgia, were always fit company, on my good days and my bad. Daphne Harvey drew my attention to an important biographical article on Marlowe, for which I am grateful; and Jack Harvey, novelist and mariner, fired my interest in Marlowe's connections with the sea. May I express my fealty and obeisance to the late, lamented King's Arms crew: Lian Hee, Stuart, Peter, Tony, Mike, Jessica, Hans, and Ian.

Vivien Chan Wai Yen was a most able and industrious research assistant and much of the tedium that comes with writing any book fell to her (sorry, Vivien).

As ever, I count myself blessed in my wife, Moira, and in my children, Odette, Alistair, Conor, and Piers. They've had to put up with a lot during the writing of this book and they did so patiently, if not silently.

Clayton G. MacKenzie
Kowloon Tong
October 2010

Introduction

The turbulence and misfortune of Christopher Marlowe's life has sometimes detracted from his importance and achievements in a most remarkable period of England's theatrical history. F. S. Boas (1953) wrote the first substantive modern biography of Marlowe, and interest in the details of the playwright's muddled affairs and in the curious and untimely nature of his death has inspired non-fictional and fictional accounts, among them those by Peter Whelan (1992), Anthony Burgess (1993), Judith Cook (1993), Robert DeMaria (1999), Lisa Hopkins (2000), Charles Nicholl (2002), David Riggs (2005), Sarah L. Thomson (2006), and Elizabeth Bear (2008). Part of the allure of Marlowe's story is the sense of intrigue that permeates almost every aspect of his life—from the nature of his political and religious beliefs to the motives for his killing. The term "subversive" provides an apt *inscriptio* for Marlowe's brief career. Marginalized by his sexual orientation and his unorthodox religious views, and possibly bound in a web of espionage, the daily path of Marlowe's life must have required subtlety, guile, obfuscation, and lies. Though we cannot presume that the strategies a writer deploys in everyday life will be reflected in the plays he writes for a paying audience,

Marlowe's awareness of the world around him and his willingness to adapt or even invert images familiar to his contemporaries may reflect a subtlety and subterfuge that had been well-rehearsed in his daily affairs outside the theater.

In our own age, and with the benefit of literary hindsight, we tend to see Marlowe's star as clouded by the greatness of Shakespeare but it would be wrong to think that this view prevailed in the early 1590s. By the time of Marlowe's death in 1593, Shakespeare (who was only two months younger than he was) had written nothing to rival the psychological intimacy of *Doctor Faustus* or the military grandeur of *Tamburlaine* or the moral brinksmanship of *Edward II*. So dazzling was his intellect that it is easy to forget that Marlowe's writing was designed not for some rarified coterie of academics but for the ordinary men and women of London. Mostly poor and illiterate, they flocked in the thousands to see his plays. Even *The Massacre at Paris*, today often dismissed as a lackluster oddity, was astonishingly successful in its first two seasons, easily eclipsing its nearest rivals *Titus Andronicus* and *The Taming of the Shrew*. The first showing in January 1593 at the Rose Theatre in Southwark grossed £3 and 14 shillings—the highest take for any play of that season and almost three times the average seasonal rate for a performance (Poole 4).

What was it that drove the popularity of Marlowe's plays? This book is in large part my response to that question. My argument is that Marlowe drew widely—much more widely than is presently thought—on the visual diversity of his age. The low literacy rates of sixteenth-century England supported a highly visual society in which images (tavern signs, flags, tapestries, church ornaments, murals, clothing, book emblems, and all manner of everyday objects) were more central conduits of meaning for the ordinary person in the street than the written word. Marlowe, as a playwright creating visual tableaux on stage, could rely on a common understanding of a rich array of visual knowledge. He could count on the fact that his audience would appreciate the significance of the *danse macabre*, of Fortuna and her wheel, of doom murals, of *morte et amore* woodcuts, and of England's paradisaical mythology. If he could do this, then he could also manipulate the meanings of relevant images, imbuing them with subtleties of significance that work beyond the literality of words spoken on stage. This presented Marlowe with an immensely powerful tool and he was not alone in exploiting its possibilities. In the nineteenth century Henry Green documented many hundreds of emblematic allusions in Shakespeare's plays and the fashion of referring to the emblem books, that most popular of Elizabethan and Jacobean literary hybrids, is discernable in a wide range of period works.

Marlowe differs from most of his contemporaries in both the control and the development of his visual patterning, and in his willingness to experiment with iconic and emblematic resources. While for many dramatists such allusions were a way of connecting with the audience, of harnessing their attention and affirming a commonality, Marlowe's manipulation of visual resources often seeks to challenge or extend the thinking of the playgoer. His method is daringly experimental. In the earlier plays, *Dido, Queen of Carthage* and *Tamburlaine*, he seems to be testing his powers, almost abandoning himself to the vogue of profuse emblematic and classical allusion that was flaunted as a sign of worldliness by many writers of the 1580s and 1590s—not least by Shakespeare in the *Henry VI* trilogy. With *The Jew of Malta* and *Edward II*, however, visual allusions become more restrained and subtle. The emphasis is no longer on impressing but on expressing. In the first of these plays, Marlowe shows himself interested in developing the idea of self-mythologization or, more accurately, erroneous self-mythologization, using the vehicle of popular *picturae* and iconography. In the second, *Edward II*, this experiment turns itself into an intricate and coherent scheme of English self-mythologization in which bogus mythmakers rise and fall as a tragicomic preamble to the emergence of the true English mythmaker. It is my argument that *Doctor Faustus* and (yes, controversially) *The Massacre at Paris* see Marlowe at the acme of his manipulative powers. *Doctor Faustus* is a consummate psychological study and one that is underpinned and undermined by highly subversive emblematic schemata. *The Massacre at Paris*, I submit, is a beautifully sculpted parody of the *danse macabre*, drawing its visually literate audience into a pointed debate about the meaning of government and power and life itself.

Marlowe's drama is suffused with death—from the carnival of savagery that parades through *The Massacre at Paris* to the scythe-bearing Mower of *Edward II*. Skeletal death, in its several artistic guises, is preeminent amongst the images of mortality that the drama unwraps. Death figures stalked their prey on almshouse walls and on teaspoons, in book margins and snuffboxes, in churchyards and on chancel arches. There were other representations of death, too, some subtler and some more sympathetic. Whatever their form, Marlowe seems to have been drawn ineluctably to the iconography of death, more so than any other dramatist of his lifetime with the possible exception of Thomas Kyd. Though influential and popular, Kyd's *The Spanish Tragedy* offered a mangled Virgilian opening and a train of ghostliness, revenge, and horrific murder that was designed to conjure extravagant fear. As a consequence, Kyd's writing feels overwrought and unrestrained. It laid him open to parody and Shakespeare, Jonson, and Marlowe duly obliged. It is intriguing that Marlowe's *The Massacre at Paris*, perhaps written within a couple of years of Kyd's play, has itself been the subject of intellectual deprecation, with one critic dismissing it as "a series of meaningless violent acts" (Kirk 193). As I have suggested already, nothing could be further from the truth. The visual patterns of *The Spanish Tragedy* are all too often inconsistent, struggling to support the innovation of the play's conceptual plan. But Marlowe's play, in contrast, is masterly in its imagistic execution, offering a theatrical animation of the dance of death and subverting its traditional meaning into a powerful political statement.

Each of the six central chapters of this book will focus on one of Marlowe's plays. Though an agreed ordering of the plays is yet to be established, I have mostly followed the date of composition suggested in Mark Thornton Burnett's edition of *Christopher Marlowe. The Complete Plays* (1999).[1] Burnett is undecided on a date of composition for *Doctor*

Faustus, offering both 1588–1589 and 1592–1593. Support for a 1588 dating of the A-Text has come from several sources including David M. Bevington and Eric Rasmussen[2] but I still hold with Hilary Gatti's belief that "most modern commentators are agreed that [*Doctor Faustus*] is Marlowe's final work" (74). In the absence of decisive evidence one way or the other, and given the extraordinary accomplishment of the play, a dating of 1592 seems the more persuasive option.

Dido, Queen of Carthage (c. 1585–86) was published after the dramatist's death. The publisher, Thomas Woodcock, attributed the text to both Marlowe and Thomas Nashe. The matter of dual authorship has left the play in what Godshalk calls "a kind of critical Limbo" (1). Although it is probably the earliest of Marlowe's plays, exactly how early it is remains a matter of debate. If Marlowe began writing it during his university years, then it may have coincided with the later courtship period between Elizabeth I and François, Duke of Anjou (1579–81). This would enhance the possibility of a parallel between the Elizabeth–Anjou flirtation and the liaison between Queen Dido and her wandering foreign suitor. Even if the play was written half a decade later there might still have been dramatic mileage in stirring up the hot political embers of Elizabeth's courtship. Something of Marlowe's method is evident in the series of dramatic vignettes that draw on popular Renaissance images of Cupid, Venus, and Death. In the opening acts of the play Marlowe seems to rebuff the traditional representations of love in the emblem books, resisting the temptation to talk of Dido's love in terms of fire, danger, death and violent passion. In the case of fire, this seems all the more peculiar because it offered so many tantalizing connectors—the fire that destroyed Troy, the funeral pyre at the end of the play. It is only when Dido and Aeneas have consummated their love in a forest cavern that the imagery of love suddenly assumes the destructive nuances so persistent in the emblem books. In the shadows and distorted shadows of familiar emblems—particularly the *morte et amore* woodcuts popularized in England by Andrea Alciati, Geffrey Whitney, and others—Dido and Aeneas act out their tragedy, slipping between comedy and pathos, substance and shadow, and even life and death itself. Marlowe's play moves beyond a simple discussion of love and its dangers and into a subversive and dangerous realm, one that explores the fine line between personal preference and political duty.

The *Tamburlaine* plays (c. 1587) are more complex in their manipulation of visual images than *Dido, Queen of Carthage*, but equally willing to maneuver familiar emblems to political ends. Their overtly militarist context seems to have encouraged the dramatist to explore a wider range of emblematic and iconographic materials relating to death. Marlowe's achievement in these pieces, as many critics have averred, is to set up an edifice of superlative humanity while at the same time undermining the very foundations of that construct. I approach this old theme from a relatively new angle—the emblematology of death that resonates through both plays. By appropriating popular visual *picturae* and developing them into dramatic visual emblems, Marlowe offers his reader simultaneous and competing narrative discourses. Tamburlaine's glory comes increasingly to be viewed through the ironic vistas of the emblem books. More than this, and as in the later play *The Massacre at Paris*, Marlowe is able to press these significances into a broader, more politicized debate. With Elizabethan England standing on the cusp of its own vast empire, and the envious eyes and swords of its countrymen turned towards their European competitors and the riches of foreign lands, what checks and balances stand between justice and tyranny? Empire demands the subjugation of Others—of their identities, of their rights, of their lives. But what if the audience could be made to sympathize with the plight of these subjugated Others? What if they could be presented not as Others but as sentient, intelligent human beings? How would that change things and what would it say about the whole matter of empire? The questions are engaged as Marlowe's manipulation of death images draws his playgoers to the edge of a vast and bleak abyss, and invites them to stare into the diverse possibilities of England's future.

The Jew of Malta (c. 1590) would have suggested to an Elizabethan audience very clear moral divides between Christian and Muslim, and

Christian and Jew. Certainly, Barabas plays to that design with a litany of crimes that would have done any serial killer proud. He is, it is true, the victim of prejudice and misdoing but everything about him points to a *But might* man who should not prosper. At the outset his alliance to Machevill and Fortune casts upon him the mantle of bad-doing and misjudgment, and sets him firmly on the road to disaster. Barabas, for example, attributes his personal wealth to God and Fortuna. In so doing he convolutes an iconic dichotomy (between Fortuna and God) that was widely understood in Marlowe's day—and one that found popular statement in contexts as diverse as the walls of Rochester Cathedral and the pages of Whitney's *A Choice of Emblemes* (1586). At the moment of retribution, and to general surprise, Barabas falls into a boiling cauldron that is suddenly discovered on stage. As he pleads vainly for help, the dramatic tableau of his suffering resonates powerfully with the murderers' pot of *yes* medieval doom mural paintings. In the Chaldon mural, just south of London, the devils dunk their wards with unerring zeal and take time to gloat on victims and potential victims. As Ferneze gloats on his foe the Jew, he announces to all and sundry that bad deeds warrant appropriate punishments. He assumes a choric role here, drawing on Barabas's own words to damn him and scorning the Jew's efforts to control fortune and devise his own fate. The problem is that in doom mural eschatology this is exactly the function assumed not by the righteous but by the devils themselves. Is Marlowe's wry subversive humor at work again, and are we in some sense meant to read Ferneze as akin to a doom mural devil, dunking a murderer in the boiling cauldron and reminding us of our earthly obligations—but actually bearing no greater moral propriety himself than the victim he torments?

In *Edward II* (c. 1592), the dramatist's experimentalism draws away from the subject matter of earlier plays and addresses a theme that is rather more visionary than visual. For the Elizabethans "paradise" was an evocative term, redolent of an island fortress protected by a silvery sea and spangled with a glorious history of military conquest. Integral to this encomium was the idea that the spirit of English monarchial glory was *C /*

reaffirmed and reborn from generation to generation, thus defying the reality of physical death. The view is most famously summarized in John of Gaunt's English panegyric in the second act of *Richard II*:

> This blessed plot, this earth, this realm, this
>   England,
> This nurse, this teeming womb of royal kings,
> Fear'd by their breed, and famous by their birth,
> Renowned for their deeds . . .
>   (2.1.50–53)[3]

On the face of it, *Edward II*, Marlowe's first and only dramatic engagement with overtly English subject matter, would seem to promise little of the paradisaical. Nonetheless, Marlowe carefully marshals the imagistic descriptors of the English paradise, demonstrating how Edward II and the time in which he lived fell so regrettably short of mythological expectations. In so doing, Marlowe invests into a succession of characters the rhetoric of the English mythology, allowing each to presume, briefly, the mantle of mythmaker before extinguishing his or her pretensions. In this chapter it will be argued that the passing parade of bogus mythologizers, enflamed with the words but not the true substance of the English mythology, is set up as a deliberate counter to the emergence of the genuine English myth maker, Edward III, at the end of the play. Aside from Elizabeth I, no English monarch was held in greater estimation than Edward III and his presence in the closing scene of the play comments pointedly on the nature of myth-making and kingship.

The *Massacre at Paris* (c. 1592) at first seems remote from English concerns but quickly reveals itself to be an extension of some of the key issues that Marlowe developed in *Edward II*. Once typified as anti-Catholic propaganda and dismissed as the remnants of a garbled or pirated copy of the original, more recent studies have positioned *The Massacre at Paris* as a more subtle and even subversive theatrical piece. My chapter argues that the episodic form of the play, embracing a pattern of brutal murders laced with black humor, is suggestive of the *danse macabre*—and that this association contributes to the subversive resonances of the text. In the *danse macabre*, originally a form of theater popularized in late medieval France, a number of actors representing a cross-section of humanity, from king to pauper, would appear on stage.[4] Death figures would emerge and one by one the earthly representatives would be dragged off to the grave. They may struggle, argue, or plead but for each the certainty of death was unavoidable. In *The Massacre at Paris* a range of victims from school-teachers to cardinals is assailed by groups of witty murderers, controlled by either the Guise or King Henry. This pattern appears to mimic the dance of death tableaux of medieval Europe. As a visual subtext, the *danse macabre*, with its emphasis on the leveling and impartial nature of death, may contend subversively with the propagandist stream that appears to run so resolutely across the surface topography of the play. The *danse macabre*, in proposing the hopeless failure of life and humanity, echoes the failure of leadership and government that we see reflected on all sides in *The Massacre at Paris*. And this, in turn, may suggest a significance that extends into the machinations of elite aristocratic politics and perhaps even into the murky, muddled world of the English ruling class itself.

Doctor Faustus (c. 1592–93) has very much the feeling of an emblem book, carrying us from place to place, from one famous character to another, from one moral issue to the next. The purpose of the play has been much discussed and what kind of morality the discourse promotes has not been uniformly agreed but, as John D. Cox has suggested, "defiance and subversion have long been suspected" (46). The impulse towards religious subversion in *The Jew of Malta* is driven to breathtakingly daring limits in *Doctor Faustus*. As the play progresses we become aware that Marlowe is consistently exploiting the visual pre-knowledge of his audience. For example, in the Diana and Actaeon "horning" caper (Act 4), Marlowe's text subverts the original meaning of the Actaeon myth and Faustus is cast in a poorer light for it. The episode thus serves as a kind of theatricalized emblem, animated on stage and carrying the heavy moral load of the emblem books. Again, in the case of Helen of Troy (Act 5) the censorious typifications of the emblem books pile even more moral impropriety on Faustus's dalliance with the Grecian queen. The impact of these nuances depends very much on the existing knowledge of the audience—a knowledge that apparently escapes Faustus's notice. But that, the play suggests, should not surprise us. Faustus, the master of knowledge, is catastrophically deprived of knowledge by the very terms of the contract he signs with the devil. Without the intellectual stimulus that necromantic knowledge could have provided, he descends into carnal instinct and crude desire. Marlowe's subversion lies in the radical conundrum that seems to present itself to the audience at the play's end: could it be that it was not, in fact, knowledge that damned Faustus's bold experiment but, rather, the *failure* to achieve knowledge that rendered it meaningless? For a man dedicated to learning and letters to have lost his soul for a pittance of pleasure is a waste indeed—but had he lost his soul for limitless knowledge and a glimpse of the mystery of divinity, would that have altered, in any way, our judgment of the play's outcome?

I have already mentioned the emblem book genre and since I draw heavily on these texts it may be worth saying a little more about them.[5] The rise of the emblem book in the sixteenth century was built on a simple success formula: pictures with verse explications. If the invention of the printing press in the 1480s had made books affordable for a mass market, it was the emblem books that gave households across Europe a reason to buy. A tripartite mix of moral adage (the motto or *inscriptio*), woodcut (the figure or *pictura*), and verse or prose epigram (the *subscriptio*), such texts appealed to a wide audience. On one hand, marginal notes about Greek and Latin verse derivations satisfied the scholarly *literati*; on the other, simple moral pictures gave meaning to those who could not read. The greatest of the sixteenth-century emblematists was Andrea Alciati whose *Emblematvm Libellvs* (1534) had appeared in more than a hundred editions by the close of the century and had spawned dozens of imitators and copiers, among them Marquale, Lefèvre, Daza, Hunger, de Bry, de la Perrière, Combe and the most celebrated English emblematist, Geffrey Whitney, whose *A Choice of*

Emblemes was published in 1586. It would be quite wrong to presume that a man of Marlowe's erudition would have relied entirely on the emblem books for his sources of information but he knew well enough that the emblem books could provide important connectors between his theater and the audience's knowledge.

Finally, a short note about the "icon" and "emblem." The term "emblem," from the Latin *emblema*, originally signified a raised or inlaid ornamentation—a sword embossed on a shield would be an emblem. In the sixteenth century, however, perhaps through association with the emblem book genre, the term frequently carries a moral and allegorical meaning, sometimes quite complex. The word "icon," from the Greek *eikōn*, signifying "likeness" or "image," overlaps to a degree with "emblem," and there is some evidence that early modern usage regarded them as interchangeable.[6] That said, "icon" may be distinguished as a broader term than "emblem." An icon could be a painting or a picture in a book, but it could also signify a statue or a monumental figure. Further, by Elizabethan times the term "icon" had acquired a distinctly religious flavor. Holinshed's *Chronicles of England, Scotland, and Ireland* (1577) observes that "The pope ment, by causing such ikons to be erected, to prefer Thomas as a perpetual saint to all posterities" (2:147). Oddly, though, the term did not necessarily carry a moral import. It could, for example, refer simply to a portrait image, as with the "*Icones* or *Portraitures*" offered in John Speed's 1611 *The History of Great Britaine* (5.7.2); or to an artifact, such as the pure gold "Icon of an elephant" that Sir Thomas Herbert (1638) saw on his foreign travels and which, to Herbert, carried no significance other than its intrinsic beauty as a piece of art (255). All this can be confusing and, as a working definition, I have therefore opted to use the term "icon" to refer to images in the broadest sense of the word, and to use the term "emblem" to describe a kind of icon that appears in an emblem book or in a book that offers images similar to those one might expect to see in an emblem book.

Notes

[1] All references to Marlowe's text are from Burnett's edition, unless otherwise indicated.

[2] Bevington and Rasmussen make their observation in a note to line 1.1.98 of their edition of the A-Text *Doctor Faustus* (1604). My study focuses on the 1604 version since most scholars, though not all, hold this to be the version closest to that which was performed in Marlowe's lifetime.

[3] All references to Shakespeare's text are from *The Riverside Shakespeare*, ed. G. Blakemore Evans et al.

[4] The origins of the *danse macabre* are by no means certain and few texts have ventured to engage this artistic *topos* in the format of a full monograph. Drawing on the early work of Francis Douce (1833) and Emile Mâle (1909), James M. Clark's learned study *The Dance of Death in the Middle Ages and the Renaissance* (1950) stands as perhaps the most persuasive authority on the subject. Clark defines the dance of death thus:

> By the Dance of Death we understand literary or artistic representations of a procession or a dance, in which both the living and the dead take part. The dead may be portrayed by a number of figures or by a single individual personifying Death. The living members are arranged in some kind of order of precedence, such as pope, cardinal, archbishop, or emperor, king, duke. (1)

Clark uses this distinction to adduce that the dance of death is a medieval invention since classical representations of skeletons do not show them integrated with the world of the living (2). Drawing on research undertaken by Mâle, and from a range of fragmentary early sources, Clark suggests that the origins of the *danse macabre* may have been in drama, the earliest example of which was possibly a dance of death masque or *tableau vivant* produced at Jedburgh, Scotland, in 1285 (93). An ancient account of the entertainment at this event (a royal wedding) gives some credence to the supposition. At any rate, Clark argues that an accumulation of evidence (91-94), ranging across half a dozen significant sources, is sufficient "to establish the fact of a Dance of Death drama and to prove its priority as compared with the pictures" (94). A number of writers have investigated specific connections between the *danse macabre* and pre-Reformation theatre. Elina Gertsman (2006) has written extensively about the medieval performance of the dance of death and Sophie Oosterwijk's (2002) exploration of the *danse macabre* in relation to the Chester mystery play cycle concludes that, by the second quarter of the sixteenth century, "Death had long been a familiar stage figure in morality plays" (287).

[5] The importance of these texts to Renaissance literary studies was persuasively established in Rosemary Freeman's *English Emblem Books* (1948). Arthur Henkel and Albrecht Schöne's *Emblemata: Handbuch zur Sinnbildkunst des XVI. und XVII. Jahrhunderts* (1967) was the first major assemblage of Renaissance emblems.

[6] John Bossewell, for example, refers to the print of a bird as an "icon" in *Workes of armorie, deuyded into three bookes* (1572).

Chapter 1. Love, Death, and the Corruption of Meaning in *Dido, Queen of Carthage*

Dido, Queen of Carthage was published by the London bookseller Thomas Woodcock the year after Marlowe's death. The title page apportions authorship jointly to Marlowe and the talented but less prodigious Thomas Nashe. The driving force for the publication of this quarto edition had come from Nashe himself and his input into the play has been much debated. The early critic Ronald McKerrow questioned whether he "had much or any share in the composition" (295), while H. J. Oliver is one of a small but illustrious line of dissenters to this view (xxii–xxv). By and large, recent criticism holds that while "divided authorship is widely presumed to be more likely than not" (Merriam 425), Nashe's contribution is "generally agreed to have been minimal" (Jackson 258). Even so, the presence of a second name on the title page has muddied critical waters. William Leigh Godshalk, who also doubts the contribution of Nashe, concedes that the double attribution "forces the scholarly critic to be less than confident about the genuinely Marlovian qualities of the poetry" (1).

Recent criticism, though, has put these qualms aside and brought into focus some intriguing readings of the play. Margo Hendricks, reminding us of Elizabethan obsessions with Troy and the idea that the British race had descended from that great civilization, argues that the play's concern with England's Trojan heritage was an attempt to "reinvent" England as an imperial inheritor: "sixteenth-century England had neither an indigenous imperial history to draw upon (as did, for example, the French with Charlemagne or the Italians with the Romans) nor an existing hegemonic history (as Spain did with its control of its extensive territories outside its geographic boundaries to proclaim itself an empire)" (165). Marlowe's representation of the Carthaginian queen, Hendricks suggests, "valorizes an emerging cultural tendency toward reductive caricatures of both women and Africans" (174), offering a prophetic warning of the racism and prejudice that threaten to hallmark England's nascent imperialism. Emily C. Bartels prefers to see the play as a study in the building of empire, arguing that Marlowe's subversive destabilization of familiar constructs serves to challenge imperial aspirations and to expose "the demonization of an other as a strategy for self-authorization and self-empowerment" (xv). For Bartels, Marlowe's greatest subversion is "not the characters' or the playwright's identification with the alien but the insistence that such an identity does not, of itself, exist" (13). On the matter of empire, Donald Stump has also noticed the undermining inclinations of the play, offering a detailed analysis of some of Marlowe's deliberate deflations of the *Aeneid*. He demonstrates persuasively that the play offers a "relentless travesty" (94) of Virgil's original and goes on to speculate that the playwright intended a shadowing of the feckless Aeneas with the equally self-serving and inconstant Duke of Anjou whose proposed marriage to Elizabeth I was being touted at roughly the same time he believes Marlowe began writing the play (98). Stump surmises that the work exposes the human failings and foibles that "inevitably compromise even the noblest aspirations to empire" (103).

What seems to me intriguing about these three interpretations is that each in its different way identifies a process of subversion in which Marlowe puffs up cultural and literary stereotypes and then deliberately diminishes them. To a greater or lesser extent, this pattern recurs in all of Marlowe's plays, and most notably in *Edward II*, where an English heroic archetype is several times trumpeted only to find its authenticity undermined by the detail of the unfolding drama. *Dido, Queen of Carthage* is similarly concerned with the subversion of empire and heroic Englishness but it presents such subversion through the corruption of common emblematic archetypes of love and death. It will be argued that Marlowe's theatricalization of popular cultural images serves to endorse and articulate the kinds of subversive currents that critics have identified in the drama, expressing a world view that is not only different from but in many cases opposite to the Virgilian resonances that run across the face of the play.

* * *

Marlowe's source for *Dido, Queen of Carthage* was the first four books of Virgil's *Aeneid*.[1] In Book I, addressing her son Cupid as the only one who can control the mighty power of Jove the Thunderer, Venus orders him to wheedle his way into Dido's affections and then "breathe into her invisible fire, and poison her, without her knowing" (48). This command is part of the story's scheme of well-intentioned but ultimately tragic deific interference. The idea of "poison" is reshaped in the very first sentence of Book IV: "Dido, gnawed by love's invisible fire, had long suffered from the deep wound draining her life-blood" [97]. The image of love as a consuming fire is reiterated within twenty lines ("the old fire coming near again" [97]) and a page later Dido's heart is described as "kindled, ablaze" (98). Shortly after we hear how "all the time the flame ate into her melting marrow, and deep in her heart the wound was silently alive" (98). Virgil then describes how "Poor Dido" roamed the city distraught, her heart "afire" (99). Mortally wounded by Cupid's barbed arrow, she wanders with "the deadly reed fast in her flesh" (99) and soon we are told the "maddening poison" of love has seeped into her very bones and that "she is ablaze with love" (99). All this occurs before Aeneas has any mind to deceive Dido or run for his ships, before even the thunderstorm has separated the pair from their companions and allowed them to consummate their love in a forest cavern (102).

In the equivalent story span of Marlowe's play not once is Dido's love linked with images of poison or fire or dissolution or fatality. This I find odd, given that the *Aeneid* makes so much of the associations. You might have thought, too, that Marlowe would have been enticed by the delicious imagistic possibilities of connecting the fire of Love with the inferno of Troy and the funeral pyre at the end of the play. Not a bit of it. Only when Dido and Aeneas are in the cave together does the Queen suddenly reach for a (sexualized) image of fire and urgency in an effort to prod her unwitting companion into action:

> DIDO: Aeneas, O Aeneas, quench these flames!
> AENEAS: What ails my Queen? Is she fall'n sick of
>   late?

> (3.4.22–23)

Marlowe's stolid and un-Virgilian Aeneas may misunderstand the Queen's words but no one in an Elizabethan audience would have displayed such ignorance. The connection between Cupid and fire was reiterated in works as diverse as John Harrington's "Sonnet on Isabella Markham" and the airs of Thomas Campion. It appears in a contemporary song "Tho the young prize Cupid's Fire," of unknown authorship, and in the lyrics of numerous ballads of the age. Visually, it was one of the most enduring themes of popular art in mid- to late sixteenth-century Europe, with a stream of emblematic and iconic representations making the connection between fire and Cupid's destructive power axiomatic. Andrea Alciati, preeminent amongst sixteenth-century emblematists, offers just such a print titled "Vis Amoris" (the Power of Love), in which a naked child Cupid breaks a bolt of lightening in two, thus putting Jove the Thunderer firmly in his place

(*Emblemata*, emblem 108). The theme was reiterated by Marquale ("Forza d'Amore," emblem 95) and Hunger, the latter attaching the following explication (translated from the German): "Little Cupid breaks a thunderbolt with his arrow and his fire. This shows that love has such great heat that no power can withstand it" ("Krafft der Lieb," emblem 78). These themes of Love's fiery dangers also appear in Guillaume de la Perrière's *Le Theatre des bons engins* (1544)—a popular work in Marlowe's day and one that had appeared in English translation by the time of his death. In print 79 (see fig. 1), a blindfold Cupid heats a fire with bellows. The heart in the midst of the fire represents the affections of a lover. Above the fire, in an alchemist's still, the water of tears is being distilled. The verse adage reveals how ardent love often turns to tragedy and warns the reader that love has hundreds and thousands of dangers ("des dangers à millier & à ces"). In Achille Bocchi's *Symbolicarum Quaestionum*, Cupid looks on dispassionately at the woman he has just mortally wounded (Bk. 1, symbol 7, 18–19). Flames spurt violently from the arrowhead buried deep in her chest. Geffrey Whitney's *A Choice of Emblemes* (1586), the most celebrated if not the first of the English sixteenth-century emblem books, offers a print titled "Potentissimus affectus, amor" (Love, the most powerful of emotions), in which the reader is advised that Cupid is so dangerous he is best avoided altogether (63).

I can only think that Marlowe's unusual representation of Dido's love in the first three acts of the play is deliberate. He was a gifted Latinist and had produced an outstanding translation of Ovid's *Amores*, probably while still a student at Cambridge University (Gamel 2). Donald Stump's authoritative study confirms that Marlowe's grammar school and university curricula had "immersed" him in the study of Virgil (86). And Marlowe's manipulations of the Virgilian original in other respects reveal him as a man who knew his source text intimately. It seems to me likely that Marlowe understood precisely the tenor of Virgil's representation of Dido's love and that for the first half and more of his own work he deliberately stripped away the implications of danger and poison and fire. It is as though he wished to convey to his audience

Figure 1. "The Dangers of Love." Guillaume de la Perrière's *Le Theatre des bons engins* (Paris: Denis Janot, 1544), fol. L4ᵛ. The alembic distillation of human love results in a flow of tears, here seen pouring from the spout on the right. Reproduced with the kind permission of the University of Glasgow Library, Department of Special Collections.

the extreme naïveté of Dido (and with it her extreme vulnerability). Once Aeneas has made clear his intentions to abandon her, she quickly adopts typically Virgilian characterizations of Cupidian love:

> These words are poison to poor Dido's soul.
>> (*Dido*, 5.1.111)

> What gods be those that seek my death?
>> (*Dido*, 5.1.128)

> Wilt thou now slay me with thy venomed sting . . . ?
>> (*Dido*, 5.1.167)

> If he depart thus suddenly, I die.
>> (*Dido*, 5.1.209)

> For I intend a private sacrifice,
> To cure my mind that melts for unkind love.
>> (*Dido*, 5.1.286–87)

How all this connects to Marlowe's wider intentions in the play is intriguing. Whether Marlowe began writing the play during the later courtship period between Elizabeth I and François, Duke of Anjou (1579–81), as Stump speculates, or in the aftermath of that courtship (c. 1585), as Mark Thornton Burnett's dating suggests (*Complete Works* xii), the encounter between the English queen and her French suitor would still have held sufficient dramatic charge to spark the interest of those in an Elizabethan audience whose political acumen was subtle enough to make the connections. The Duke was twenty-two years her junior and there is evidence to suggest Elizabeth was very fond of him and took his marriage advances seriously. When he stayed in her palace, she brought him beef tea each morning and bestowed upon him a richly jeweled toque. According to Leonie Frieda, she referred to him as her "frog," confiding that he was "not so deformed" as reports had suggested (397). For a time she took to wearing an earring in the shape of a frog (Somerset 408). Elizabeth's proposed marriage caused uproar amongst

England's Protestant majority and engendered widespread disapproval. The queen reacted with fury to criticism, meting out draconian punishments to those who wrote or spoke against her, including the severing of hands (MacCaffrey 243–66).

Several critics have identified a relationship between Dido and Elizabeth, not only in Marlowe's play, but also in the wider art and literature of the age. For many reasons, it was an attractive association—but it could also be construed negatively. In Marlowe's *Dido*, it seems to me, the character and development of Cupidian imagery moves to support the contention by Deanne Williams (31–60) and others that Dido is Elizabeth. Dido's infatuation with Aeneas is driven with a force that makes her oblivious to the dangers involved. In the face of criticism from her own people, and despite the growing derogation of her duty as monarch, she persists in desperate endeavors to make the Trojan prince her husband. We don't really know if Elizabeth's liaison with Anjou ever reached the point of desperation, or if even it amounted to anything more than political posturing on her part, but in the popular Protestant imagination, marriage to Anjou was a real threat—just as it was the spectacular hope of England's secretive Catholic minority. Marlowe's imagery presents a queen who flies in the face of a significant body of popular opinion. If Dido is meant to represent Elizabeth, then the English queen is presented as vulnerable, misguided, hapless—and dangerously seeking to temper forces that will inevitably wreak destruction upon herself and her country. And if this association is true, then by corrupting and reconstructing the force and focus of love imagery in Virgil's *Aeneid*, Marlowe signals a movement from naïve innocence to painful experience, from an ignorance of Cupid's ways and wiles to a deadly understanding of the consequences of Love.

* * *

The connection between Dido, Elizabeth, love and misjudgment may perhaps be pressed just a little further. There is brief mention of an aged nurse in Book 4 of the *Aeneid* but she says nothing and carries neither the significance nor the duties of the Nurse in *Dido, Queen of Carthage*. The character and words of Marlowe's Nurse are entirely his own invention. At the end of Act 4, she seems to hint at one of the most popular and recognizable emblems of the sixteenth century:

> NURSE: Say Dido what she will, I am not old;
> I'll be no more a widow, I am young;
> I'll have a husband, or else a lover.
> CUPID: *[disguised as Ascanius]* A husband, and no
> teeth?
> NURSE: What mean I to have such foolish thoughts!
> Foolish is love, a toy. O sacred love
> If there be any heaven in earth, 'tis love,
> Especially in women of your years.
> Blush, blush for shame, why shouldst thou think of
> love?
> A grave, and not a lover, fits thy age.
> A grave? Why? I may live a hundred years:
> Fourscore is but a girl's age; love is sweet.
> My veins are withered, and my sinews dry;
> Why do I think of love, now I should die?
> (4.5.21–34)

The presence of disguised Cupid turns the old Nurse's thoughts to love. At first she is defiantly triumphant; she's not old but young and a husband is what she needs. Cupid pretends consternation: a woman with no teeth and seeking a husband? The thought cows her and defiance turns to shame. It is a grave her age demands, she muses, not a lover. Then she again reviews and revises her opinion. Eighty years isn't *that* old—why, chance may be that she will live to a hundred. Why shouldn't she fall in love? At the root of this shifting self-debate lies the conundrum that mystifies her: Why do I think of love, now I should die?

In 1586, Geffrey Whitney published an emblem titled "De Morte, et amore: Iocosum" (132) in which two drinking partners, Cupid and Death, mix up some of their arrows after a heavy night out. For this reason, Cupid occasionally kills his victim and Death occasionally makes his fall in love: "That age did loue, and youthe to graue did goe" (132). In Whitney's image a young man lies dead while an old man, arrow in his back, walks with a handsome woman. Published in 1586, Whitney's woodcut would have been hard pressed to have influenced Marlowe's play but this story of Cupid and Death had a long emblematical pedigree. Andrea Alciati, the most famous of the sixteenth-century emblematists, first popularized the image in 1534, suggesting that both Cupid and Death were blind companions who accidentally switched some of their arrows while they were hanging out together (*Emblematum Libellus*, emblem 155). In his cut, a young man lies dying while an old man grapples friskily with a reluctant maiden. The dying youth speaks: "Spare me, [Cupid]; and you, Death, holding the symbols of victory, spare me: / Let me love, make the old man go down to Hades" (emblem 155).[2]

Alciati's youth asks to be spared by both Death and Cupid. The image was repeated and often pirated, with minor variations, in numerous works of the age, finding a place, too, in some highly influential emblematical publications, such as those of Wolfgang Hunger (1542, emblem 66) and Giovanni Marquale (1551, emblem 137). Whatever their source, the emblems are virtually uniform in making the point that Love and Death are beyond mortal control. The quivers of Cupid and Death represent a fundamental principle of instability; their arrows may strike in the most unlikely of places and with the most unpredictable and tragic of consequences. Many emblematists—Whitney and Alciati among them—advise that Cupid's arrows should be avoided altogether. This theory is promoted in Shakespeare's *Romeo and Juliet* when Romeo explains why the fair Rosaline will have nothing to do with him:

> . . . she'll not be hit
> With Cupid's arrow, she hath Dian's wit;
> And in strong proof of chastity well arm'd,

From Love's weak childish bow she lives uncharmed.   *Magic,*
(1.1.208–11)   *possession*

Her object is to live "uncharmed" (the 1597 first quarto reads "unharmed") and, in doing so, she follows the advice of the emblem books. Avoid love; avoid Cupid. It is a dreary truth but one that Rosaline studiously observes. She survives.

Elizabeth I was in her early fifties by the time Marlowe had finished writing *Dido, Queen of Carthage* but that was a goodly age in a time when the average life span was less than forty. It seems conceivable that an incorrigibly subversive Marlowe may have fashioned his Nurse as a further warning to the Virgin Queen, a reiteration of the potential frailties and fatalities of Cupid's love. Perhaps he even intends us to see in the Nurse something of the Queen herself as she courted the youthful Duke of Anjou, a man many years her junior. When the Nurse invites Cupid (disguised as Ascanius) to go to her house, her image of a fruit-laden garden is reminiscent of Tudor paradisaical conceptions of England:

> No, thou shalt go with me unto my house.
> I have an orchard that hath store of plums
> Brown almonds, services, ripe figs, and dates,
> Dewberries, apples, yellow oranges;
> A garden where are bee-hives full of honey,
> Musk-roses, and a thousand sort of flowers,
> And in the midst doth run a silver stream,
> Where thou shalt see the red-gilled fishes leap,
> White swans, and many lovely water-fowls.
> Now speak, Ascanius, will ye go or no?
>
> (4.5.3–12)

England as paradise is something I shall return to in my chapter on *Edward II* but it's worth mentioning here that the notion of England as a well-tended garden—as in the Gardener's scene of *Richard II* (3.4)—was highly accessible to the Elizabethans. Joshua Sylvester's translation of Du Bartas's work, titled *His Diuine Weekes and Workes* (1578), frames England as "Europes Pearle of price, / The worlds rich Garden, Earths rare Paradice" (462). Centuries before, Geoffrey of Monmouth's *Historia Britonum* (dated in the first half of the twelfth century by G. H. Gerould [34]) had explained the reasons why the Trojan Brutus was attracted to the country: "The name of the place was Albion and only a few giants lived there, no one else. Deserted as it was, it was an attractive place, with many rivers abounding with fish and beautiful forests" (20).

Twice the Nurse encourages Cupid into her home, enticing him with the bounties of her well-tended garden. If in this paradisaical vignette there lies a metaphor for England's garden, then the implications for England's queen are urgent. Just as the Nurse misinterprets the nature of her young guest and misunderstands the powerful emotions she so willingly embraces, so, too, Elizabeth's affections for the Duke of Anjou may be courting catastrophe for herself and the country she rules.

* * *

Tim Carroll's 2003 production of *Dido, Queen of Carthage* at Shakespeare's Globe in London focused on Cupid as the hilarious young master of mayhem. Cupid, played by the actor James Garnon, was presented as an amateurish archer, pursuing first Dido and then the Nurse with admirable zeal but mixed results. When the arrows hit, the infatuations of love thrived; when they missed, sanity prevailed. The order of the world became a matter of comic lottery—and yet it was a lottery behind which moved one very clear certainty. Avoid love and the precarious consequences of love are also avoided. If a person could choose not to fall in love, or could suppress private emotions to a greater cause, then he or she might find a shield against the connivances and dangers of Love's progress. But who could live to these exacting standards, and who would want to? The figure of Aeneas is perhaps the partial answer to that conundrum. Marlowe's play offers us little reason or inclination to like Aeneas as a man but as a missionary he may have offered London period audiences something more than he offers us. Here is the man whose legendary descendant, Brut, would found the British race and build its greatest city which even in the time of Marlowe was still referred to as Troynovant or New Troy. Aeneas is crass, wooden, insensitive, stupid, Marlowe seems to tell his peers, but without him how would you measure your own place in history? Who would you be—or would you *be* at all?

While Marlowe's negative presentation of Aeneas is reasonably constant throughout, he shows much greater inclination to manipulate our feelings about Dido. We are initially compelled to measure her naïveté against the powerful, plotting female deities of the play's beginning. And then we are invited to witness her victimization, not only through the cruel treatment meted out to her by Aeneas but also through the way her language alters and the familiar howl of a forsaken, tormented lover settles upon her speech. Having brought Dido's love for Aeneas to its consummation, the dramatist reconstitutes the imagery of love in its familiar guise—it is fiery and poisonous, it is the stuff of dissolution and death. The change is dramatic and were it not for the fact that she slips into the role of Love's victim—a guise that the cultural consciousness of an Elizabethan audience would have found believable— her passion could almost be dismissed as a caricature. But caricature it is not. This is the desperate, decimated Love of the emblem books. Whatever sympathies the play elicits, Marlowe encourages the audience to invest them in Dido. It is she who has given all and received nothing, and she whose future has been sacrificed so that the destiny of the British race may thrive.

Whether Elizabeth I saw *Dido, Queen of Carthage* is unknown and the date and venue of the first performance of the play are equally uncertain. No doubt there were men of influence, voices at Elizabeth's court, who saw early performances of this play and reflected upon its implications for a queen who seemed bent on a foreign marital match. It must have struck disquieting chords as well with ordinary educated Elizabethans who were only too aware of the Duke of Anjou's brutal and mischievous forays in the Low Countries—a train of such bloody mismanagement that even his mother, Catherine de Medici, is reported to have lectured him for six hours in March 1578 on the errors of his ways (Sutherland 205). English isolationism, summarized neatly in John of Gaunt's panegyric in *Richard II* (2.1), did not reach out instinctively to embrace foreigners, and certainly not those with the Catholic adornments of the Duke of Anjou. The warning to Elizabeth seems stark and unequivocal. As the less-than-admirable Aeneas submitted callously to a different and greater destiny, so, too, England's Eliza, an altogether more glorious and worthy leader, must nonetheless submit to the same principle. The consequences of not doing so are abundantly evident in the personal ruin of Dido and the imminent destruction of her realm.

Notes

[1] There were translations of the *Aeneid* available in the late sixteenth century (such as Gavin Douglas's 1513 Scots edition) but Marlowe's skill as a Latinist, affirmed most recently by Mary-Kay Gamel, suggests he would have read Virgil in the original (613–622). For ease of reference I have used W. F. Jackson Knight's fine translation in all references to the *Aeneid*.

[2] The translation here is provided in *Andreas Alciatus 1: The Latin Emblems, Indexes and Lists*, ed. Peter M. Daly.

Chapter 2. *Tamburlaine* and the Masks of Death

The striking presence of death imagery in the *Tamburlaine* plays has drawn comment from a number of critics. Susan Richards suggests that Tamburlaine has attained "the ultimate power in terms of human life— the power of giving death, which is the essential power of the warrior-emperor, the cause and result of his position" (375). Herbert B. Rothschild, Jr. observes that "Marlowe repeatedly raises our expectation of Tamburlaine's overthrow and death only to defeat that expectation" (63). Stephen Greenblatt calls Tamburlaine "a desiring machine that produces violence and death" (195). While *Dido, Queen of Carthage* relied heavily on cautionary *picturae* of love and death, the military world of *Tamburlaine*, with its brutality and sadistic fantasy, demanded a more shocking and pointed set of images. Marlowe found these in the icons and emblems of skeletal Death that terrorized the walls and parchments of medieval and early Renaissance Europe, a ubiquitous statement of mortality's earthly preeminence and a reminder of the ephemeral nature of all human life.

Tamburlaine openly associates himself with the figure of Death. Here he is in Act 5 of *Part One*, with the Virgins of Damascus at his mercy:

> Your fearful minds are thick and misty, then,
> For there sits Death, there sits imperious Death,
> Keeping his circuit by the slicing edge.
> But I am pleased you shall not see him there;
> He is now seated on my horsemen's spears,
> And on their points his fleshless body feeds.
> Techelles, straight go charge a few of them
> To charge these dames, and show my servant Death,
> Sitting in scarlet on their armèd spears.
>
> (*Part One* 5.1.110–18)

In describing Death as "my servant" Tamburlaine could have in mind at least two mythopoeic scenarios: one classical, the other Christian. In classical terms, Death was the servant of Mars Ultor, the god of war. This point is noted in Vincenzo Cartari's highly popular *Le imagini de i dei de gli antichi* (1556, sigs. 11$^{r\text{-}v}$)—a text reprinted many times and in several languages, including English, before 1600. There is certainly a link between Tamburlaine and Mars in the plays but it is infrequent and fluctuating. For example, in Act 4 of *Part One* he espouses his loyalty to the god of war but within a few minutes has reversed the image, styling himself as Mars ("The god of war resigns his room to me" [5.1.451]) and demanding that "grisly Death" (456) should do "ceaseless homage" (457) to his sword. In *Part Two*, Mars is barely mentioned. It is a moot point as to whether all of this represents inconstancy on the part of the playwright or whether it is intended to be symptomatic of Tamburlaine's increasingly unstable character.

The Christian connection is perhaps more fruitful. In sixteenth-century biblical terms it is God who controls Death. The point is reiterated in any number of period texts, among them the play *Everyman* (2. 64–79), and it was certainly a *sine qua non* in visual representations of skeletal Death, or the "fleshless body" as Tamburlaine calls it. For this reason, grinning skeletons graced the walls of sixteenth-century churches and cathedral settings across Europe. These icons reminded those who viewed them that this—the skeletal image—is what *they* would come to be. Like Hamlet looking upon the skull of Yorick, they were unwittingly looking upon themselves. Death was all part of God's plan. It was inevitable and the joys of heaven or the torments of hell would be judged by deeds performed on earth. To the man or woman who had cherished mortal things at the expense of piety there was every reason to be filled with abject terror at the approach of Death. But for those who had spent their lives in the pursuit of goodness, or whose suffering had ripped from them all joys of mortal existence, why should not Death be welcomed? As part of his self-mythologization, Tamburlaine interprets Death as bloody, brutal, skeletal, and obedient to his whims. This, in part, is his vision of empire; this is the kind of death that inhabits his heroic landscape. It is not a fully coherent scheme—images merge and separate. At some points Tamburlaine is the mediator between Life and Death, at others the master of Death, and elsewhere Death itself. This tentative, shifting symbiosis is perhaps indicative itself of a man who is drafting the terms and conditions of empire before our eyes.

* * *

While the imagery of Death is mapped out mostly volubly in the words of Tamburlaine, other characters assert world pictures in which Death is clothed in a more desirable guise. In fact, one of the first images of Death we meet in *Part One* is neither bloody, nor brutal, nor skeletal. When, in Act 2, scene 1, Cosroe envisions the death of his foolish brother, King Mycetes, he does so in terms that suggest an expiry of the gentlest sort:

> And when the princely Persian diadem
> Shall overweigh his weary witless head
> And fall like mellowed fruit, with shakes of death,
> In fair Persia noble Tamburlaine

> Shall be my Regent and remain as King.
>   (Cosroe, 2.1.45–49)

This is a wonderfully soft image, reminiscent of a scene carved on the alabaster columns of the early sixteenth-century de la Warr Chantry in Boxgrove Priory, West Sussex. Here a maiden gathers fruit while a *carving* young man, her lover perhaps, perches high in the tree shaking the branches. The fall of ripened fruit encompasses a process of accommodation and timeliness and comfortable death. Cosroe pictures a harmonious collaboration with Tamburlaine, one in which his own views of succession and gentle mortality prevail. That Cosroe thinks all this possible is part of his delusion, but also an illustration of the "newness" of a persona like Tamburlaine—the persona of superlative military superman. The Elizabethans were used to the ideas of black intrigue and political maneuvering, but the all-conquering, all-compassing nightmare of a Tamburlaine was fresh territory for them. Like Cosroe, they had never encountered, or even envisioned, the kind of empire that a man like Tamburlaine might construct. And like Cosroe they may have supposed that Tamburlaine would observe the etiquettes and mores of succession and regal compromise. As he lies wounded and dying, five scenes after visualizing his gentle cameo of monarchy and mortality, Cosroe's overwhelming mien is one of surprise:

> And Death arrests the organ of my voice,
> Who, entering at the breach thy sword hath made,
> Sacks every vein and artier of my heart.
> Bloody and insatiate Tamburlaine!
>   (*Part One* 2.7.8–11)

In two sentences he concedes everything: the failure of his own monarchical myth and the savage preeminence of Tamburlaine's empire. He is, for all intents and purposes, a dance of death victim, staring with terror into the hollow eyes of Death. Death "arrests" his voice as if it were a policeman arriving at the scene of a crime to bring him to account. And more than that, Death loots the veins and arteries of his life. Print 7 in Hans Holbein's *Imagines Mortis* is titled "The Emperor" and offers a startling parallel to Cosroe's situation (see fig. 2). In Holbein's print, skeletal Death grasps the crown of the emperor with one hand and with the other reaches inside the emperor's head, as if disassembling the very organs of life. *Imagines Mortis* was published in Lyons in 1538 under the title *Les Simulachres & Historiees faces de la Mort, avtant elegammet pourtraictes, que artificiellement imaginées* and the production of a third edition in Latin in 1542 confirmed its cross-European importance. Many other images from this text remind us of Cosroe and, in each case, the arrival of death is marked by a sense of astonishment or indignation.

"Bloody and insatiate Tamburlaine!" curses Cosroe, and he chooses his words tellingly. Tamburlaine's empire will bring not only death but also an "insatiate" lusting for death and the full host of barbarities that might accompany it. Mark Thornton Burnett, among others, has explored the patterns of bodily mutilation that run through both plays, suggesting that "Opening up his foes . . . is not enough for Tamburlaine, and he inflicts upon them other hallmarks of the 'grotesque'" ("Tamburlaine and the Body" 35). But why travel to such grotesque lengths? Why unleash the tyrannies of death? Surely, they are not driven by the desire for honorable reputation? Lisa S. Starks has contended that they bear the marks of Tamburlaine's "sadistic fantasy" (183); and perhaps more tellingly Johannes H. Birringer sees them as "the violent fantasies of unconditional power" (130). The truth may be that Tamburlaine does these things because he *can*, because the nature of empire is such that it risks losing or forgetting the checks and balances that ordinarily would prevail. In this respect he reminds his audience of the animated skeleton of the *danse macabre* who delights in the pointless torment of victims before the moment of execution.

It may well be that Marlowe has transfigured the Death figures of Renaissance art into tyrannical emblems of empire. The acquisition of empire inevitably required military conflict and there are many sixteenth-century examples of images encompassing both skeletal Death and battle. Hans Holbein's cut of a knight skewered by a lance-bearing Death is

*Dispone domui tuæ, morieris enim tu, &
non viues.* ESAIAE XXXVIII.
Ibi morieris,& ibi erit currus gloriæ tuæ.
ESAIAE XXII.

*Sic tibi disponas commißi munera regni,
Vt transire alio posse repente putes.
Cur? quia cùm uitam suscepta morte repones,
Tunc tua diuulsus gloria currus erit.*

Figure 2. "The Emperor." In this extraordinary print an emperor dispenses justice and wisdom as Death delves casually into his skull, perhaps reaching for the very mechanism that controls life and being. From Hans Holbein's *Imagines Mortis* (Lyon: Ioannes et Franciscus Fellonii, fratres, 1545), fol. A6^r. Reproduced with the kind permission of the University of Glasgow Library, Department of Special Collections.

perhaps the most notorious of these (see fig. 3). Claude Paradin's skeletal Death in *Les Devises Heroiques* appears ecstatic as he prepares to slay a soldier who pleads for mercy (172b). His hollow skull is angled not towards his victim, but towards the audience, smiling. On one level he is reminding all those who watch to change their ways. But, on another, the picture is an exercise in sadistic voyeurism. The excitement of killing, written in the rapture of the skeleton's face, is heightened by the sense of audience. A similar print in Vincentio Saviolo's *His Practise. In two Bookes* (1595), on the subject of battle, reveals a ragged Death skeleton bragging to a knight on horseback and pointing to a grim cadaver that lies near by. Again, in one sense he is offering the knight a warning about the death that awaits all men and women but in another he revels in his cruelty and in the feeling of audience that the passing knight bestows.

* * *

Reporting to the Soldan, the messenger of Act 4, scene 1 of *Part One* describes Tamburlaine as the universal mower:

> Black are his colours, black pavilion,
> His spear, his shield, his horse, his armour, plumes,
> And jetty feathers menace death and hell,
> Without respect of sex, degree or age,
> He razeth all his foes with fire and sword.
>
> (*Part One* 4.1.59–63)

He conceives of Tamburlaine as the Death-dealer who plies his trade amongst young and old, poor and rich, male and female. Here is exactly the thesis of skeletal Death in Holbein's *Imagines Mortis*, and yet the messenger's picture is incomplete. Like the messenger, Tamburlaine may see himself as the universal, irresistible foeman whose will may not be assuaged ("This is my mind, and I will have it so" he says at 4.2.91 in *Part One*) but given the tyrannical world he has shaped, marked by repeated cruelties and suffering, is death such a bad option after all? Could it even

Subito morientur, & in media nocte turba-
buntur populi, & auferent violentum
absque manu. IOB XXXIIII.

Insurgent populi contra fera bella gerentem
Qui nihil humanæ commoda pacis amat.
Magnanimo freti uiolentum robore tollent,
Ipse cadet nulla percutiente manu.
Nam genus humanum ualidis qui læserit armis,
Auferet hunc fato MORS *uiolenta graui.*

C 2

Figure 3. "The Knight." Death skewers a knight with his own lance. The knight flails his sword gamely but what match is this for the shock and awe of Death? From Hans Holbein's *Imagines Mortis* (Lyon: Ioannes et Franciscus Fellonii, fratres, 1545), fol. C2^r. Reproduced with the kind permission of the University of Glasgow Library, Department of Special Collections.

be desirable? John Donne's sonnet "Death, Be Not Proud" scorns the cruel poverties of death, mocking Death as a thing as transient and fragile as mortality itself: "One short sleep past, we wake eternally, / And death shall be no more; Death, thou shalt die" (2. 13–14).

With characteristic mischievousness, Marlowe works through this issue from an Islamic rather than a Christian angle. Tamburlaine's Muslim foes aptly represented the distant and exotic Otherness that the term "empire" conjured in the Elizabethan imagination. They were perfect subjects for a study on the human consequences of empire. On the face of it, they had nothing at all to do with Marlowe's England, and yet is not empire defined in some sense as the conquest of people who have nothing at all to do with their conquerors?

We learn little from Tamburlaine's high-status Persian and Turkish prisoners. Cosroe comes and goes quickly; one of his primary functions is to signal the rise of a force and an attitude that is unfamiliar to the world he knows. Marlowe's treatment of Bajazeth and Zabina is more extended and ambivalent. Their amazement at Tamburlaine's disregard for degree and status (3.3.225–26; 4.2.58–59) is reminiscent of Cosroe and their treatment at the hands of Tamburlaine manifestly more barbarous. Yet somehow they fail to find a firm niche in the audience's affections. In performance Bajazeth's final speech lends itself as an expression of what Jonathan Burton calls "ample nobility" (130), and certainly his self-inflicted death is the stuff of pity—but not, curiously, pathos. Certainly, the declamatory, hyperbolic nature of Bajazeth's speech, conjoined with virulent anti-Christian invective and a pompous litany of threats, would have done little to endear him to an Elizabethan audience. And Marlowe invested scant effort in rehabilitating Bajazeth, following his source closely (Foxe's *Actes and Monuments*) and giving credence to William J. Brown's assertion that "As Marlowe does later, Foxe portrays Tamburlaine's harsh treatment of Bajazeth with complete sympathy and approval" (41).

If Marlowe maintains a casual emotional distance between Bajazeth and the playgoer, the same is not true of Alcidamus, King of Arabia. Within minutes of Bajazeth's suicide, Arabia (affianced to Zenocrate) appears on stage, wounded and at the edge of death. Up to this point we know very little about him. Agydas tells us he is young (*Part One* 3.2.57), the Soldan tells us he is fair (4.1.68), and Arabia himself has uttered a mere fifteen unremarkable lines. An ill-guided young man who, in sum, speaks much more about love than he does about war, Marlowe's drama at least partly cossets him with our sympathies:

> Then shall I die with full contented heart,
> Having beheld divine Zenocrate
> Whose sight with joy would take away my life
> (5.1.418–20)

Then, a dozen lines later, Arabia surrenders himself to the comfort of Death:

> Since Death denies me further cause of joy,
> Deprived of care, my heart with comfort dies
> Since thy desirèd hand shall close mine eyes.
> [*He dies.*]
> (5.1.431–33)

Arabia is content to die, even desirous of death, for distinctly non-spiritual reasons. Having been robbed by approaching death of the world's joys and its cares, Arabia declares himself to be happy at the sight of his beloved Zenocrate and her apparent safety and at the thought that she will close his eyelids in the moments following his death. The contentment with death is a visual and tactile contentment, a recollection of touch and sight and a projection of a companionship for a brief space beyond the boundary of physical life. This celebration of the joys of earthly love is unusual but not without precedent in medieval and Renaissance funereal monuments. Aside from the maiden who gathers fruit and a young man who shakes the branches, the marble columns of the de la Warr Chantry at Boxgrove Priory are showered with Cupids—a paean to earthly life that neatly conjoins the ideas of youth, temptation, and death. And in Chichester Cathedral the tomb of a knight and his lady holding hands in the most affectionate and casual of ways, a posture celebrated in Philip Larkin's poem "An Arundel Tomb," celebrates not a life to come but a life that has been. Here is no commemoration of the vermiculation of the grave or of the ethereal reconstitution of spiritual being. On the contrary, this is mortal life in its most cherished guise, something that is both valued and intrinsically valuable.

It is one thing to choose heaven over mortality but quite another to prefer the "nothingness" of death over earthly life. The joys and sorrows and hopes of Arabia are all clasped in those few moments before physical oblivion. His death is an indictment of what has become under Tamburlaine's sway a mutilating and annihilative world. Nonetheless, while we may sympathize with Arabia, his sense of Otherness is only partly diminished by his longing for the nothingness of death. While many an Elizabethan could empathize with the earthly vitality of the de la Warr chantry, few could comfortably step so far as to conceive of death as a finality of nothingness. Surely *something* lay beyond the grave? To sixteenth-century thinking it is Arabia's atheism that deprives him of the fullest humanity and, therefore, of the fullest sympathy.

Marlowe waits until *Part Two* to press the experiment that final step further. There, Olympia—Muslim wife of the Muslim Captain of Balsera—proposes suicide to her son. She has just seen her husband die from bullet wounds and fears that she and her son will soon perish cruelly at the hands of barbarous Scythians. Olympia envisions a destiny in heaven, asking the "God of heaven, / [To] purge my soul before it come to thee!" (3.4.32–33). The Death she envisages is not at all the fearsome scavenger of the emblem books:

> Death, whither art thou gone, that both we live?
> Come back again, sweet Death, and strike us both!
> One minute end our days, and one sepulchre
> Contain our bodies, Death, why com'st thou not?
> 　　　　　　　　　[*She draws a dagger.*]
> Well, this must be the messenger for thee.

> Now, ugly Death, stretch out they sable wings
> And carry both our souls where his remains . . .
> (*Part Two* 3.4.11–17)

It is not grief at the death of her husband that drives Olympia's desire for death but rather the fear of the torments that may be inflicted on her and her son by their captors. Death as an escape from physical torture was a well-established maxim in Marlowe's day. Recalling the brutalities of the sixteenth-century Catholic Inquisition, James Morice, in *A briefe treatise of Oathes exacted by Ordinaries and Ecclesiasticall Iudges* (1590), notes that the "lengthe of torture suceeded in taking from Death his due title of King of terrors, and making him a welcome friende, that endes so manie miseries" (156).

The idea of desirable death as an escape from the trials of mortal life constructed a lesser-known but distinctive *topos* in Renaissance art. It is perhaps best illustrated in the work of Georgette de Montenay, one of the few known female emblematists of the sixteenth century. In one print (emblem 89) an affable skeleton helps an elderly man who willingly steps out of a symbolically hollow world (see fig. 4). The comforting, dainty hand he lends to the old man casts him in the guise of a carer rather than of a demonic slayer of mortality. A Latin motto, "desiderans dissolvi" (the desire for dissolution), is written in the clouds above the old man's head. So, too, Arnold Freitag in *Mythologia Ethica* (1579) represents Death, arrow in hand, as he advances mercifully on an over-burdened traveler (11). Even Holbein offers a cut (print 33) in which an old man is assisted calmly to the grave by skeleton Death. There is nothing fearful or gloating about this species of Death. On the contrary, his coming is to be welcomed, desired even.

What is interesting about Olympia's longing for death—and what distinguishes her from the King of Arabia in *Part One*—is that she preserves some sense of religious decorum. She asks death to "carry both our souls where [her husband's] remains." She believes in an afterlife, in a destination for souls, and in the possibility of post mortal reunion.

Figure 4. "Desiderans Dissolvi" (The Desire for Dissolution). Georgette de Montenay's cut of skeletal Death helping an old man in *Emblematvm Christianorvm Centvria* (Zurich: 1571), fol. B1ʳ. Uncharacteristically, Death is here represented as a caring assistant, helping the old man to step out of an empty, hollow world. Reproduced with the kind permission of the University of Glasgow Library, Department of Special Collections.

Olympia is a Muslim but her repudiation of physical life and her celebration of spiritual life could easily be encompassed by that most Christian of Renaissance emblematists, George Wither: "Death is no Losse, but rather, Gaine; / For wee by Dying, life attaine" (emblem 21; see fig. 5). Whatever her religious persuasion it is her humanness that Marlowe draws from the tableau of her suffering. The world of death is attractive to her because it gives her the opportunity to recover the things that empire has destroyed—family, happiness, togetherness, human tenderness. These are all qualities that an Elizabethan audience, or any audience for that matter, would have admired. In longing for "sweet Death," then, Olympia draws on a discreet but discernible tradition of Death as a liberating friend rather than an aggressive foeman. And in so doing she disengages herself from the sense of Otherness that empire has imposed upon her and becomes no different to those—the playgoer, you and me—who mourn for her.

* * *

When Tamburlaine speaks of a "Shaking and quivering" Death who "flies away at every glance" (*Part Two* 5.3.68, 70), he opens up the seemingly unthinkable possibility that Death itself is conquerable. The idea that Death may be assuaged or deferred or pacified was a *non sequitur* in the letters of medieval and Renaissance Europe. Holbein's "The Pedlar," for example, reveals a salesman, knapsack on his back laden with goods, at the very moment he is seized by Death (print 37; see fig. 6). He tries to argue but death will have none of it. However, philosophers and *cognoscenti* alike suggested that there were intellectual or spiritual ways of "defeating" death. The road to piety, as expressed in John Donne's "Death, Be Not Proud," leads to the eternity of heaven and, in a sense, represents the conquest of a Death who holds sway only over things ephemeral—"Death, thou shalt die," as Donne puts it in the last words of the poem. This, of course, required full religious belief. To those lacking such heightened piety, and enamored of earthly life, it was small consolation. Another possibility presents itself in the first illustration

Figure 5. "Death is no Losse." An emblem of life and death, reiterating the idea that physical death is merely the gateway to spiritual life. The image is packed with *memento mori* elements, from the sprigs of wheat growing through the skull's eye sockets to the scythe-bearing harvester in the background. From George Wither's *A Collection of Emblemes, Ancient and Moderne* (London: 1635), 21. Reproduced with the kind permission of the University of Glasgow Library, Department of Special Collections.

Figure 6. "The Pedlar." Death interrupts a pedlar whose wares are strapped to his back. The victim seems to suggest he needs a few moments longer to sort out some matter or other but his skeletal assailant is unsympathetic. From Hans Holbein's *Imagines Mortis* (Lyon: Ioannes et Franciscus Fellonii, fratres, 1545), fol. C5ʳ. Reproduced with the kind permission of the University of Glasgow Library, Department of Special Collections.

in Wither's *A Collection of Emblemes, Ancient and Moderne* (1635), which reveals the mirror image of a scholar on one side of a tree and skeletal Death on the other (21). On the side of the scholar, the tree is full of leafy life; on the side of Death, the branches are bare and barren. The emblem's motto reads "By Knowledge onely, Life wee gaine, / All other things to Death pertaine," suggesting that the accumulation of knowledge (which may be passed on as a body of learning to future generations) is another way of defeating Death.

But how could a soldier like Tamburlaine, noted neither for his piety nor for his learning, conquer Death? William Wyrley, a celebrated Elizabethan military commentator, suggests that fame itself may defeat mortality:

> True golden fame, blacke death cannot defile,
> Glistening honor buds from dustie graue,
> Ech noble Lord that beareth glorious stile
> Spend most his life eternall praise to haue.
> (58)

[handwritten margin note: Ultimately an illusion]

Everlasting fame has been a traditional compensation for death, and it is a theme that finds statement and restatement in the work of Shakespeare and his contemporaries. Yet when Wyrley speaks of "Glistening honor" that "buds from dustie graue" we have to wonder just how much glistening honor there is in Marlowe's *Tamburlaine* plays. Sarah Emsley suggests that "Even when characters believe they are using the word honour to mean 'noble conduct,' their speech is continually undermined by their actions" (173). Lisa S. Starks notes that "Tamburlaine's sadism . . . is obvious in his aggressive desire to break laws, torture victims, kill virgins," arguing further that Tamburlaine believes in "a kind of 'moral' structure in the universe, an inversion of traditional moral order in promoting evil in its purest form" (180). No honor here then.

Tamburlaine's achievements may not have earned him honor in the chivalric sense of that word but certainly he has found an enduring historical and military (and even theatrical) niche. His own sense of immortality, though, seems to reach much further than this. Refuting the possibility that death can ever touch him, he declares: "Sickness or death can never conquer me" (5.1. 220). David H. Thurn offers the intriguing insight that Tamburlaine "creates a delusional space in which absolute sovereignty becomes possible" (5). Within this delusional space it is conceivable that Tamburlaine believes he will never die. Coming at a moment of such pointed physical weakness, the assertion reminds us of the vain defiance of emperors and kings in the passing parade of the medieval *danse macabre*. The claims of invulnerability, the appeals for exemption, the statements of defiance—all compose the litany of misapprehension that typifies the end of earthly pomp. Tamburlaine may claim "a close relationship to the gods" (131) as Roger E. Moore puts it, but it is not quite close enough to avoid death.

As this truth dawns on him, Tamburlaine begins to concede ground to his physical mortality:

> See where my slave, the ugly monster Death,
> Shaking and quivering, pale and wan for fear,
> Stands aiming at me with his murdering dart,
> Who flies away at every glance I give,
> And when I look away, comes stealing on.
> Villain, away, and hie thee to the field!
> I and mine army come to load thy bark
> With souls of thousand mangled carcasses—
> Look, where he goes! But see, he comes again
> Because I stay. Techelles, let us march,
> And weary Death with bearing souls to hell.
>   (*Part Two* 5.3.67–77)

The image of a tentative, unconfident death "Shaking and quivering, pale and wan for fear" is not one that is familiarly portrayed in the emblem books. A 1592 woodcut in Theodore de Bry's *Emblemata* reveals a faithful lover bringing a rose to his slightly bashful skeletal bride or lover (n.p.). A variation on this theme appears in the Parish Church of St. Mary

Magdalene at Newark-on-Trent where a shy early-Renaissance cadaver, her legs splayed in the customary antic disposition of the *danse macabre,* offers a carnation to the suavely dressed young man in the panel next to her. But these are images of coyness, and neither suggests the evasion or intimidation of death. Pierre Coustau, in *Le Pegme de Pierre Coustau* (1560), presents the image of Death as fleeing from a human pursuer (214). Death looks back as he runs, perhaps hesitant but still smiling, the accompanying verse advising "La mort ne peut payer tribut ne taille, / Necessité ne permet que l'on donne" (214)—suggesting that this is not, in fact, an image of Death on the run but a metaphor for his lack of accountability. While the domestication of death, as revealed in the somewhat amusing Elizabethan tribute to John Thomas Hylocomius in St. Alban's Cathedral, is not uncommon, the idea that Death may be rebuffed or hectored is rare in the art of the age. Revered by those he tutored, Hylocomius was commemorated by his students in a mural on the south aisle of the Cathedral. He is represented as a jolly-looking skeleton reposing on a bed after his long years of work. There is something distinctly affable and non-threatening about the representation in keeping with spirit of those his pupils who loved him.

Tamburlaine's image of hesitant Death is peculiar not only with regard to the iconography of Marlowe's day but also with reference to the imagery of the *Tamburlaine* plays themselves. Death has dallied in the folds of Tamburlaine's brows (*Part One* 2.1); it has arrested Cosroe's voice (*Part One* 2.7) like the sergeant death who arrests Hamlet in the last act of Shakespeare's tragedy; it has perched precociously on the spears of Tamburlaine's horsemen (*Part One* 5.1); and it has granted Olympia relief from the pain of life (*Part Two* 3.4). Now, suddenly, Death is afraid and hesitates to assail great Tamburlaine. This tentative, timorous Death occurs in other sixteenth-century drama. In Beaumont's *The Knight of the Burning Pestle*, Death is caricatured by Rafe as a kind of scallawag inventively trying to drum up business by mischievously slipping into a shop wearing a tradesman's blue apron in order "To cheapen *Aqua-vitae*" (5.3.155) before fleeing under the protection of a cloud of pepper. There is also an interesting account of "fallible" Death in Shakespeare's *Richard II* when the king is murdered in the Tower of London:

> *The murderers [Exton and servants] rush in [armed].*
> KING RICHARD: How now, what means Death
>   in this rude assault?
> Villain, thy own hand yields thy death's instrument.
>   [*Snatches an axe from a Servant and kills him.*]
> Go thou and fill another room in hell.
>   [*Kills another.*] *Here Exton strikes him down.*
> That hand shall burn in never-quenching fire
> That staggers thus my person.
>   (5.5.105–09)

The dance of death *topos* is here transformed into a dramatic animation, offering both dramatic spectacle and embedded meaning.[1] Death, the great leveler, has come to seize a victim—in this case a king—who will be reduced to dust like any other mortal being. But what we have here is more than a simple mimetic process. Richard slays two of his "Death" attackers, an outcome uncharted in the standard iconographies of the dance of death. Has Richard conquered death in some sense by slaying a theatricalized emissary of the *danse macabre*? Has his courage and ingenuity postponed, however temporarily, the preordained moment of his passing—the moment, as Gilles Corrozet tells us in *Hecatongraphie* (1543), that none of us may know or change (Niiii [*sic*])?

The same questions may be asked of Tamburlaine but the answers are equally uncertain. As Tamburlaine sees Death approach and retreat, arrow in hand, he acknowledges that he is in the thrall of skeletal Death and his efforts to assuage and weary Death by providing him with a surfeit of alternative corpses savors of the desperation that animates human faces in death murals across Europe. There is some consolation, though. Death at least pays him the compliment of a measured campaign rather than a rough, brutish assault—stalking him with guile and caution, wary that this is no ordinary prey.

Tamburlaine's life ends with the much-discussed words "Tamburlaine, the scourge of God, must die" (5.2.249) but in a line laden with ambiguity, it is unclear whether the "must" is a rueful admission or a statement of determination. In attempting to elude physical death, he has first tried to fight off his skeletal adversary, then claimed that he will rule in a better, ethereal place, and finally affirmed that he will survive through his sons. All of these signify, as Susan Richards has noted, that Tamburlaine lacks "the perception of man's limitations—even that most irrevocable of his limitations, his mortality" (387). And this, she contends, denies the play the fullest sense of tragedy. Certainly, the arrival of Death brings to Tamburlaine no great illumination or insight, as Sir Walter Raleigh supposes it should (117). In the end, he may lay claim to only the slenderest of advantages: that of all the deaths that occur in these plays, his is among the more comfortable. If Marlowe has not entirely reaffirmed the standard moral and religious aphorisms of the *danse macabre*, the play at least ends with the tacit affirmation that, after all is said and done, the greatest of earthly monarchs is still Death himself. At the close, Death stands as a simple variation on the invincible adversary of the emblem books, unusually tentative and unnerved, as is fit for a foeman of mighty Tamburlaine, but equally indefatigable and ultimately irresistible.

* * *

In the 1580s England stood on the cusp of empire, and yet Marlowe wrote *Tamburlaine* a decade before the East India Company, the greatest trading company in history, had been formed. Jonathan Burton makes the valid point that in 1579 when England established formal relations with Ottoman Turks—upon whom Tamburlaine vents his militarist spleen—it occupied no colonies or territories outside the British Isles and was "a bit player on the world stage, a latecomer seeking a niche in a mercantile economy which had left it behind" (130). It is hard to believe that Tamburlaine's apparition of empire would have sat any more easily on the minds of a period audience than it does on our own. Elizabethan literatures abound with images of positive kingship, images that compare cruelty and vindictiveness unfavorably with compassion and tolerance. Geffrey Whitney's *A Choice of Emblemes* (1586), the most important and persuasive of the sixteenth-century emblem books, has a great deal to say on the appropriate and inappropriate powers that rulers may exercise over those around them. In "Pietas in patriam" (111) a king is commended for sparing the life of a worthy opponent; in "Impar coniugium" (99) the wicked (and, it seems, apocryphal) ruler Mezentius is reviled for executing his opponents by tying their living bodies to the corpses of plague victims. The moral implication of these and other emblems is that a monarch's duty is to respect the sanctity of human life and to rule with control and compassion.

At a time when England was nucleating its own imperial ambitions, the lesson on empire was apposite. On the one hand, the prospect of empire provided the Elizabethan imagination with a limitless canvas for its seething ambitions. Paradoxically, it was at once a way of asserting England's rising pride and of dispelling the insecurities of leadership and isolation that had plagued it since the accession of Elizabeth I. On the other hand, empire ventured into untrammeled psychological space and it risked, as Tamburlaine reveals only too well, the dangers of psychopathic excess. Marlowe's drama tells us that the idea of empire is glorious but that the design of empire can easily misfire. Marlowe manipulates emblems of skeletal Death in order to iterate these contending thoughts. It is in images of Death that Menophon first articulates the awesome progress of Tamburlaine:

> His lofty brows in folds, do figure death,
> And in their smoothness, amity and life;
> About them hangs a knot of amber hair
> Wrapped in curls, as fierce Achilles' was,
> On which the breath of heaven delights to play,
> Making it dance with wanton majesty . . .
> (*Part One* 2.1.21–26)

He is the death dealer, the force that arbitrates the flux of mortality. Yet, like Death, who lords victory and cruel treatment over the conquered, his majesty is a "wanton majesty," subject to cruel excesses.

As Tamburlaine journeys deeper into empire, he becomes increasingly dislocated from the Elizabethan model of humane monarchy so vigorously championed by Whitney and his contemporaries—among them Shakespeare who ensures that virtually all his tyrant rulers are soundly punished for their misdeeds. As Tamburlaine's actions become less restrained, Marlowe deftly turns the image of skeletal Death against him. The exotic Otherness of Tamburlaine's Muslim foes provides the dramatist with the perfect subjects for his experiment in empire. These were the people who constructed the human matter of empire itself. The Elizabethan audience did not know them, did not understand them, did not particularly like them. But did that mean the audience could not sympathize with them, feel for them, mourn their passing? Marlowe uses images of skeletal Death to anchor our perception of Arabia and Olympia as human beings rather than the faceless booty of war. The ruin of their lives, wrought by the machine of empire, has transformed the terror of Death into the relief of Death. In her longing for "sweet Death" (*Part Two* 3.4.12), Olympia asserts her place in the same emblematized scheme of life and death as those who watch her. She is human as they are, and worthy of their empathy. That his Muslim victims long for the mercy of death and that his vision of empire is viewed through a blood-red film of extravagant suffering both testify to the fatal flaws in Tamburlaine's grand design. As Elizabethan England stood on the edge of its own empire, envying the fortunes of longer-established competitors, the *Tamburlaine* plays stand at once as a celebration of the potential of superlative militarism and as a stark warning against the excesses that can so easily flow from the impunities of conquest.

Notes

[1] For a fuller discussion of this scene and the issues raised by it, see Clayton G. MacKenzie, "Paradise and Paradise Lost in *Richard II*." The manner of Richard's death was widely debated by Tudor historians. Holinshed enumerates various possibilities, including the suggestion that Richard "was tantalized with food and starved to death" (quoted by Bullough 413). Shakespeare's decision to go with the idea that Richard was slain by attackers allowed him to theatricalize a well-known dance of death *topos*.

Chapter 3. "Neither to fate, nor fortune but to heaven": Barabas and the Route to Resolution in *The Jew of Malta*

The first sentence Barabas utters attributes his most recent profits to the "Persian ships" (1.1.2) which have brought the merchandise that he has since turned into the gold before him. His latest argosy is traveling from different points on "our Mediterranean Sea" (1.1.47), as Barabas refers to it, and a few seconds later a Merchant arrives to report "Barabas, thy ships are safe / Riding in Malta road" (1.1.49–50). But in fact not all the ships are safe; the ship from Alexandria is unaccounted for and the Merchant reports grave misgivings amongst other sailors about the vessel: "They wondered how you durst with so much wealth / Trust such a crazed vessel, and so far" (1.1.79–80). These fears Barabas immediately dismisses out of hand. He knows the ship and its strength, he says—and yet, the Merchant having departed, Barabas privately fears for its safety. He need not have worried for within seconds a Second Merchant has arrived to announce that even the Alexandrian ship has arrived safely. Barabas celebrates the religious source of his bounty:

> Thus trowls our fortune in by land and sea,
> And thus are we on ev'ry side enriched:
> These are the blessings promised to the Jews,
> And herein was old Abram's happiness.
>
> (1.1.102–05)

There are good reasons why these sentiments might have pricked the sensitivities of an Elizabethan audience. For centuries Christian scholars had struggled to present the Old Testament as the theological prequel to the New Testament, sometimes imaging conflicts in the Old Testament as contests between Jewish and Christian standpoints. Here, now, is Barabas appropriating the benefits of the Old Testament to Judaism. As G. K. Hunter has put that, "if Abraham and the other patriarchs of the Old Testament belong to the Christian tradition, they cannot belong to the Jewish one" (216).

Aside from this theological subversion, Barabas presents a period audience with an even more scintillating challenge. Everything about Barabas's enterprise in these opening fifteen minutes of the play speaks of Fortuna, not of faith. Barabas is introduced to us by Machevill who quickly repudiates religion as a "childish toy" ("Prologue" 14). In the contorted Elizabethan misconstruction of Machiavelli, the resourceful man defined his own fate if he was able to manage the power of Fortuna successfully. In *The Prince* Machiavelli devoted an entire chapter to Fortune, crediting it with sway over half of all human affairs and advising the ambitious individual to seize fortune's gifts when they are offered. More than this, in the image of Barabas's argosies, lost and saved at sea, Marlowe imitates the late sixteenth century's most common representation of Fortuna's fickle powers, that of ships flourishing and ruined on the ocean's waves. Jan Van der Noot's popular English version of *A Theatre for Worldlings* (1569) reveals a two-masted vessel coursing through calm waters, with golden sails and silken tackle and "riche treasures" (fol. E2ʳ) in its hold (see fig. 7). In the background, the same ship founders on rocks, its opulent cargo lost to misfortune. The idea of

Figure 7. "Fortuna." Jan Van der Noot's cut representing the vagaries of Fortune in *A Theatre for Worldlings* (London: Henry Bynneman, 1569), fol. E2ʳ. One ship fares well while a second sinks beneath the waves. Sixteenth-century emblematists commonly used the idea of a ship on the sea as a signifier of the unpredictable outcomes of human ambition. Reproduced with the kind permission of the University of Glasgow Library, Department of Special Collections.

the sea as the arbiter of extravagant gain and extreme loss is emblematized again in Theodore de Bry's 1592 pictura in *Emblemata de Nobilitate et officio Heraldico* which bears the inscription "His fortvna parens illis inivsta noverca est" (emblem I, translated as "To these fortune is a parent; to those a wicked stepmother"). On one side of the image of Lady Fortuna a ship sails in calm waters; on the other side another sinks in turbulent seas and within sight of the safety of a Renaissance port.

Machiavelli understood that the reality of the human condition was both changeable and slippery, and that causality lay largely beyond the power of human control. To a degree, each of us is a prisoner of our nature or character and, as such, we are conditioned to behave or respond in a certain way to a given set of circumstances. That said, the prudent man is one who can make rational, sanguine decisions, decisions that may even run contrary to his instinct. By studying the picture of the present with meticulous care, he may construe the patterning of the future and make decisions that buffer him against the adversities of the future. For Machiavelli, then, it became possible to mitigate the impact of Fortune through knowledge and, to a degree, define one's own fate. Indeed, Marlowe's Machevill holds that "there is no sin but ignorance" ("Prologue" 15). In this regard Barabas quickly shows himself to be a rather poor student of his patron-master. The reported unseaworthiness of the Alexandrian barque, apparently confirmed by Barabas's private misgivings, suggests a lack of prudence on the merchant's part, a greed-driven blindness to the known hazards of the Mediterranean. The ship arrives and all is well but the audience knows, and Barabas knows too, that this particular success has relied not on measured judgment but on sheer good luck.

* * *

As Barabas ponders his last and most outrageous maneuver in Act 5—a bid to retain the governorship lately bestowed upon him by the Turks and recapture the affection of the Maltese Christians by betraying his erstwhile allies—he reflects upon the opportunity that now presents itself:

Begin betimes, Occasion's bald behind,
Slip not thine opportunity, for fear too late
Thou seek'st for much, but canst not compass it.

(5.2.44–46)

H. G. Rusche (261) and Samuel Schuman (234–35) both suggest that Marlowe was recalling the emblem books as he wrote these lines, and probably a specific image copied from Alciati in Geoffrey Whitney's *A Choice of Emblemes* (1586). Panofsky (72) and Kiefer (1–27) have demonstrated that by the late medieval period, Occasion and Fortuna had been conflated into one figure, the fusion assisted by the Latin term for Opportunity ("Kairos") which carries the same female gender as Fortuna. In Whitney's image the baldness of Occasion's head is much more obvious than in Alciati's original (*Emblematum Liber*, sig. A8ʳ) which ran to dozens of editions through the sixteenth century. The verse epigrams to both stress the importance of seizing a rising opportunity. Let Occasion pass and there will be no dragging her back by the hair. The aphorism is curiously Machiavellian in its import, and it seems that Barabas has understood the lesson well enough. Even in Act 1, when divested of most of his wealth, Barabas consoles his daughter Abigail by suggesting that a future "occasion" will produce the opportunity to remedy present ills:

No, Abigail, things past recovery
Are hardly curèd with exclamations.
Be silent, daughter, sufferance breeds ease,
And time may yield us an occasion,
Which on the sudden cannot serve the turn.

(1.2.240–44)

Certainly, as the play progresses Barabas shows himself ready to seize any opportunity that might advance his situation.

In fact, by Act 5, he has manipulated a rivalry between Mathias and Lodowick (2.3), maneuvered them into a fight in which they kill each other (3.1), poisoned an entire nunnery, including his daughter (3.4–6), murdered Bernardine and framed Jacomo with the crime (4.1), and disguised himself as a French musician in a plan to murder Ithamore, Bellamira, and Pilia-Borza (4.4). Such a character lends itself readily to demonization. Moreover, Stephen Greenblatt has seen Barabas as a "stock type of demonic villainy" (196), who for Marlowe's Christian audience would have been "an embodiment . . . of all they loathe and fear" (203) and Andrew Hiscock argues that Barabas and Ithamore deliberately cultivate "demonic identities" (11). This is a simple interpretation of Barabas's character and for many who patronized the theaters of Marlowe's day it may have rung true. But for those who were able to take on board the greater subtleties of the play, Barabas might have presented himself as a more complex figure. And while there is perhaps less "sympathy" for Barabas than Lloyd Edward Kermode detects (216), one cannot help but suspect that in presenting Barabas's extermination of a corrupt, fornicating, sanctimonious priesthood Marlowe is himself enjoying some kind of wish fulfillment. Barabas's ingenuity in executing his various dastardly plans is worthy of our interest if not our admiration. He has by Act 5, and in a most persuasive sense, established himself as one of those authentically manipulative "climbing followers" ("Prologue" 13) of Machevill.

When Barabas falls into the cauldron in 5.5, definitively trapped by his Christian foes, he pleads in vain to Christians and Turks alike: "O help me, Selim, help me, Christians! / Governor, why stand you all so pitiless?" (5.5.69–70). He looks and sounds like one of Fortuna's victims hopelessly pleading and desperately clinging to the falling wheel in settings that range from the medieval mural in the choir of Rochester Cathedral to the faces of tarot cards that fortune tellers shuffled on the streets of Elizabethan London. He has also literally experienced that fall to the nadir of Fortuna's wheel. As in Rochester Cathedral's medieval image of a rouged Fortuna listlessly spinning her wheel, the victim's cries for help fall on deaf ears. When Barabas realizes that none will help him, he steels himself with Machiavellian defiance and focuses instead on making those who have now vanquished him aware of just *how* clever he has been:

> Then Barabas breathe forth thy latest fate,
> And in the fury of thy torments, strive
> To end thy life with resolution:
> Know, Governor, 'twas I that slew thy son;
> I framed the challenge that did make them meet;
> Know, Calymath, I aimed thy overthrow,
> And had I but escaped this stratagem,
> I would have brought confusion on you all
>
> (5.5.77–84)

In offering his "latest fate" he has become the creator of destiny, the controller of Fortune. He brings knowledge, that axiom of Machiavellian ingenuity, to Christian and Turk alike: "Know, Governor . . ."; "Know, Calymath . . ." If only he had not fallen for the cauldron trick, oh the havoc he would have wrought! But, of course, he did fall for the trick and within four lines he is dead.

As several critics have noted, the image of the Jew of Malta, writhing in a boiling cauldron, is an intensely Christian emblem of divine punishment (Hunter 233–35; Burnett, *Complete Works* 599). The boiling cauldron itself echoes medieval schema of heaven and hell, and most prominently the celebrated "Heaven and Hell" mural (one of the so-called doom murals of medieval church art) in the Church of St. Peter and St. Paul in the village of Chaldon which lies twelve miles south of London on the celebrated Pilgrims Way (the route followed by the travelers in Chaucer's *Canterbury Tales*). On entering the church, the pilgrim's eye is drawn to the medieval altar and font, the scene bathed in the rich light of leaded glass windows. But on turning to leave, the visitor is startled by an extraordinary vision of heaven and hell, looming broad and high across the back wall of the church. It is an edifying spectacle of suffering and joy, a scheme of angels and devils, saints and sinners, unqualified bliss and unimaginable torment. In the bottom left quadrant of the mural a devil stares out at the on-looker and while he does so he stirs a boiling cauldron full of people. Other devils assist him in dunking the victims with long pitchforks. It is a piece of medieval humor. While the pilgrim walked up the aisle to admire the altar, the devil had been watching and waiting—just as the devil is always watching and waiting. Similar images of devils who look not to their immediate victims but out towards their audience are to be found in doom murals at the Church of St. Lawrence at Combe and at the Church of St. James the Great at South Leigh, both in Oxfordshire, and at the Church of St. Thomas, at Salisbury in Wiltshire. In the literatures of the time, many further examples exist, as in Gabriel Simeoni's figure of merciless wickedness in *Pvrtratvres Or Emblemes* who glares exultantly at the reader as he prepares to mutilate his victim (364). The sense of a moral and religious "lesson" is implicit to all of these images and yet we have the paradox that such timely warnings of hellish retribution are delivered by a set of demonic teachers. Curiously, the devils themselves become the advocates and arbiters of appropriate moral behavior.

The cauldron, or murderers pot as it was commonly described, was an outrageously daunting torment reserved for those who had committed the most heinous of crimes. The devil who stares out in the Chaldon mural offers a salutary and unnerving warning: this could be you, he seems to glare, so behave yourself. In fact, Ferneze is quick to point out that Barabas's punishment is "thy treachery *repaid*" (5.5.73, emphasis added) and the Christian governor wishes that the Jew had lived a better life (line 74). These judgments suggest that Barabas suffers not the arbitrary whims of Fortuna but, rather, a form of divine justice—a punishment that, in the true spirit of medieval and Renaissance eschatology, befits the unforgivable crimes he has committed.

* * *

G. K. Hunter in his seminal article on Marlowe's theology offers an image of the Chaldon mural (facing 235) but curiously makes nothing of it in the text of the essay itself. Instead, he turns his attention to two other images of murderers pots—one of the Antichrist falling towards pots with fires under them and another of a cauldron boiling the covetous in the *Calendrier des Bergers*. Neither of these images seems to comment usefully on the theatrical emblematization of Barabas's death. He is a vicious man to be sure, but it would be hard to make a case for calling him the Antichrist (and, to be fair, Hunter does not) and while covetousness is intrinsic to his nature there are surely worse things we could talk about. What seems to me interesting about the Chaldon mural is that it deploys an artistic technique that appears also in the few surviving medieval doom murals of Cambridgeshire and Oxfordshire—areas that Marlowe, who had been a student at Cambridge University, must have known well enough. I am alluding to a figure within the mural who references himself not to the events of the mural but to us, the observers of the image. In the Chaldon mural this figure, as I have suggested, is a devil who stares out at the viewer. In the Church of St. James at South Leigh, it is a devil who stands in the maw of the hell-monster, dragging a mob of lassoed sinners across the chancel arch and into the jaws of hell while casually gazing down at us sinners in the congregation below. At Combe a fleshy fiend crouches in the mouth of the hell-monster looking out and pulling a tongue at anyone who cares to look back at him. And in the Church of St. Andrew in Cambridge a devil wearing spectacles peruses a list of the damned as if he is checking to see whether or not our name is listed.

These images of connection with a viewing audience served to remind the living of the inevitable consequences of their earthly actions. No one is exempt from this process. As Governor Ferneze loads the burden of deserved punishment on Barabas, announcing to all and sundry that bad deeds warrant appropriate punishments, are we in some sense meant to read him as akin to a doom mural devil, dunking a murderer in the boiling cauldron and reminding us of our earthly obligations? He has certainly studied the words of Barabas carefully. In the very last lines of the play, Ferneze urges those present to give thanks to heaven for Malta's safe deliverance from the threats of its various foes: "So march away, and let due praise be given / Neither to fate nor fortune, but to heaven" (5.5.122–23). Neither to fate nor fortune, but to heaven.

The word "fate" is something of a rarity in Marlowe's canon but here it crops up twice in the space of forty-five lines. In normal usage, fate represented the certainty of divine planning and, as such, was the very opposite of fortune which supposed that the plan could be changed. The common inscription "Inevitabile Fatum" (Inevitable Fate) appears at the base of numerous sixteenth-century death's head images and funereal effigies, succinctly acknowledging the unavoidable conclusion of all human life. Yet though fate accounted for the broad certainties of every human life (birth, death, judgment), Renaissance theology allowed for choices of virtue and vice, good and evil, under the ambit of those overarching certainties. While some facets of existence were preordained elements such as reward and retribution may be earned or avoided according to the nature of our earthly choices. The pointedly eschatological echoes of his punishment remind Barabas and his audience of the inevitable consequences of choosing evil.

Among Barabas's many misdoings we may number his attempt to pirate the term "fate" to his own Machiavellian signification. For him it has come to mean wicked prosperity through human ingenuity and manipulation and he presents this to his audience as laudable—but in order to praise him we, like him, would have to step outside all moral and religious structures. Even when his own design has failed, Barabas still clings to the notion of his supreme intellect, anxious to have us believe that his designs have failed only by the slenderest of margins ("And had I but escaped this stratagem, / I would have brought confusion on you all" [5.5.83–84]). Those who listen are only too well aware that in choosing extravagant evil as his riposte to Christian injustice, Barabas has modified his destiny both before and after death. His belated reference to Occasion, the very antithesis of fate, confirms a bold Machiavellian belief that he can control the outcomes of his life by mastering the forces of Occasion/Fortuna through sheer supremacy of intellect. His immersion in the cauldron signifies both the volatility of fortune and the limitations of human ingenuity.

In repudiating both fortune and Machiavellian fate at 5.5.123 Ferneze seems to have Barabas's earlier allusion to his "latest fate" very firmly in mind. His rejection of Barabas's notion of Machiavellian fate and of the sway of fortune as a guiding principle of life, and his affirmation of the power and benevolence of heaven, restores the play to firm Christian ground at its close.

Or does it? When he falls in the boiling cauldron, Barabas in his panic calls for help from anyone who will listen—"O help me, Selim, help me, Christians!" (5.5.69). His supplications remind us of the many damned who beg for mercy from unrelenting demons in the doom murals of middle England. Yet despite the fact that the stage is strewn with Christian and Turkish dignitaries, and an even greater assortment of bassoes and knights, only Ferneze answers him, in a sense providing the moral foil to the sinner's vain declamations. At the close of the play, it is Ferneze again who maps the moral topography of the harrowing scene we have just witnessed. It is he who delivers the theological rationale for the brutalization of sinners, he who affirms that all crimes will garner appropriate punishments, and he who wishes that Barabas "hadst behaved thee otherwise" (5.5.74). He seems to stand as an unsympathetic, moralizing intermediary, referencing the events on the stage to the audience who has been watching them, rather like the intimidating intermediary figures in the doom murals at South Leigh, Combe and Chaldon. Yet the doom mural intermediaries—and here, perhaps, we may begin to suspect the mischievous ironies that seemed to spring so readily from Marlowe's pen—are invariably devil figures, occupying at one in the same time the paradoxical roles of evil tormentors and moral objectifiers. The theatrical emblematization of Barabas's death may be placing the Governor in the role of just such a devil. If so, then Ferneze, leader of the Maltese Christians and the play's chief espouser of Christian values, is himself subtly construed as a fiend, bearing no greater moral propriety himself than the victim he reviles.

* * *

Among Marlowe's many personal foibles and subversions, suspicions of religious heresy surfaced at several points in his life. Most notably, when he and his co-conspirator Richard Baines were accused of counterfeiting coins in Holland in 1593, Baines turned on Marlowe and submitted a note to the authorities "containing the opinion of one Christopher Marly concerning his damnable judgment of religion, and scorn of God's word" ("The Baines Note"). True, it served Baines's purposes well enough to try to distract the authorities from their interest in the lesser crime of counterfeiting but, even so, we would surely not expect a man of Marlowe's intellect and creative adventurism to hold steadfastly to the bland religious orthodoxies of his day. And perhaps this sense of personal alternativism shaped his representation of Barabas in the cauldron scene. There is something disarming about Barabas in his death throes. Surrounded by his foes, spurned as an alien and without even the faintest hint that anyone might come to his aid, he stands, his head above the lip of the cauldron, insolent and unapologetic. His early success in the play had been articulated in terms of the Jewish faith but any sign of religious acclamation is missing from the cauldron scene—curious, because with Barabas knowing he is about to die that is exactly where you might have expected it to return. Nor is he cowed by the prospect of eternity in hell. When we look to the doom mural paintings of middle England, those who are about to be shepherded into hell's fiery maw are filled with a sense of sniveling contrition. There's not a jot of humor or lip from those cooking in the Chaldon mural's murderers pot, no wry smiles or cheeky epithets. Barabas is very different. At the end, he is the crude-cut Renaissance man, the damnable Machevill brimming with ill-judged ambition and adventurism, secular, evil, unerringly cocky, but somehow estimable in his defiance.

not really. remove different [handwritten annotation]

Chapter 4. Mythologies of Death in
Edward II

The triumph of Death is a recurrent and determined theme of Renaissance iconography. The rise and fall of Tamburlaine's excesses are mapped by emblems of skeletal Death, the journey culminating in his own futile efforts to escape mortality. Tamburlaine does express the vague ambition that he will live on through his son but the comment is brief and unconvincing: "Thou wilt become thy father's majesty" (*Part Two* 5.3.185) he tells Amyras but, as the stage direction indicates a line later, the youngster tellingly hesitates to mount the emperor's chariot. The hope of a glorious succession seems dim. In *Edward II*, Marlowe's only overtly "English" play, the playwright returns to the theme of heroic inheritance as a means of eluding the physical power of Death. Here the shaping of a chivalrous heroic spirit during the course of mortal life is viewed as the means of sustaining and reanimating a glorious monarchial inheritance.

At the opening of *Edward II*, Gaveston enters reading—more accurately, re-reading—a letter that has been sent to him by the king. His spirits are filled with a "surfeit" of delight (1.1.3) because the king has urged him to return to the English court. "What greater bliss" (1.1.4), Gaveston asks, can befall him? He compares his arrival in London to that of a soul achieving paradise itself: "The sight of London to my exiled eyes / Is as Elysium to a new-come soul—" (1.1.10–11). Paradise was a stirring concept to the Elizabethans. Adventurers thought they had found their own visions of Elysium in lands as geographically diverse as Bermuda, Newfoundland, and the Low Countries.[1] These, if you like, were modern paradises, economic encomiums of opportunity and wealth. An English tradition of cartography going back to medieval times had sought the location of a different kind of Paradise—the original paradise described, variously, as the Fortunate Isles, the Hesperides, the Islands of the Blessed, the earthly Elysium, Ogygia, the Garden of Eden.[2] This archetypal "paradise"—the word itself probably deriving from the old Persian "pairidaeza" which signified a walled enclosure (Wilders 133)— had allowed an English world mired in civil war to dream of a place and a perfection that was beyond their present reach but, apparently, not beyond their ken. Through all the best authority of scientific measurement and sober reasoning, and to no one's real surprise, the English cartographers deduced that England was itself the original location of Paradise. When Joshua Sylvester in his translation of *Du Bartas* writes of England as "The Worlds rich Garden, Earths rare Paradice" (462) his superlative is neither arbitrary nor accidental for he draws on a long established tradition that equated England and Eden.

In sixteenth-century English thinking, the idea of the English paradise was underpinned by clear principles, the most important of which required the defiance of death through regenerating monarchical greatness. And monarchical greatness depended largely on the requirement of peace at home and conquest abroad. These ingredients inform John of Gaunt's English panegyric in the second act of *Richard II* where he describes England as "this other Eden, demi-paradise" (2.1.42)— "demi" in the sense of second rather than half. The defining characteristics of his paradise are a line of royal kings "famous by their birth" (2.1.52) and a chivalric history of military deeds that have been perpetrated "far from home" (line 53). But more than that, idyllic England is a safe place, its surrounding sea serving "in the office of a wall" (line 47) to keep out "the hand of war" (line 44). In essence, Gaunt's England is a land of magnificent royal lineage "wont to conquer others" (line 65) rather than itself, at once celebrating foreign triumphs and repudiating internal strife or foreign intrusion. *Edward II* almost certainly pre-dated *Richard II*, and Charney has seen it as "a model" for Shakespeare's play (40).

Be that as it may, the bed of history cultivated by Marlowe in the writing of *Edward II* does not seem fertile ground for the representation of an English paradise. It depicts a particularly vicious phase of civil war, hallmarked by appallingly weak monarchy and multiple foreign incursions into English territory. What it does have, though, is a young prince, the son of Edward II, who would emerge as one of England's royal exemplars. Edward III's reputation was unsurpassed in the Elizabethan imagination; Tudor historians lauded his exploits abroad with unfailing enthusiasm, ranging from John Rastell's populist *The Pastyme of the People* (sigs. C5^r–D3^r) to the weightier *Chronycles of Englande* (published by William Caxton). A plethora of Elizabethan works on military prowess and skills made standard reference to Edward III as the primal illustration of the heroic militaristic traits they advocated—as in William Wyrley's *The Trve Vse of Armorie* ("Princely Edward mirror of Cheualrie" [81]) and Matthew Sutcliffe's *The Practice, Proceedings, And Lawes of armes* (sig. B3^r). In addition, Edward III's kingship marked an extraordinary period of domestic peace and economic progress. His reign was in every sense the legitimate precursor to the paradise that English men and women felt they enjoyed in the Golden Age of Elizabeth I's reign.

Marlowe's play addresses the seminal descriptors of the English paradise, demonstrating how Edward II and the time in which he lived fell so regrettably short of paradisaical expectations. In essence, the defeat of death through the revival of the English heroic spirit had been neglected. With Edward's failure to measure up to the English encomium, Marlowe invests into a succession of different characters the rhetoric of the English mythology, allowing each to presume, briefly, the mantle of myth maker before demolishing his or her pretensions and aspirations. I shall argue that the passing parade of bogus mythologizers, imbued with the rhetoric but not the true spirit and substance of the English mythology, is set up as a deliberate foil to the emergence of the true English mythologizer, Edward III, at the end of the play.

* * *

When Gaveston finds in the sight of London a vision of Elysium, his words would have conjured deep-rooted resonances in the minds of his Elizabethan audience. John Michael Archer draws an explicit connection between the reference to "Elysium" and the court of Elizabeth I, suggesting that Marlowe "criticizes [the court's] compulsory heterosociality by imagining a male monarch, courted by male suitors, and threatened by over-mighty male subjects" (77). Marlowe's audience surely would have detected the familiar resonances of Eliza and Elysium but whether at this stage in the play they would have unpicked the clues to a political commentary is doubtful. Similarly, Dympna Callaghan's assertion that "there is an undeniable resemblance between Edward and Elizabeth's sovereignty" needs to be treated with some caution (283). Dennis Kay seems to stand on safer ground when he proposes that "in Marlowe's play the image of the king may be construed as a negative exemplum, being defined negatively in terms of the well established cult of Queen Elizabeth" (para. 3). Gaveston may conjure an image of Elysium but the nature of the speaker and the context of his observations would quickly have struck discordant notes with his audience. Gaveston hails from France, not England, and the silver sea that walled out Albion's foes had served most actively in keeping the French at bay. No sooner has he uttered the idea of Elysium than a devaluing shadow creeps across his words:

> The sight of London to my exiled eyes
> Is as Elysium to a new-come soul—
> Not that I love the city or the men

> But that it harbours him I hold so dear,
> The King, upon whose bosom let me die . . .
>   (1.1.10–14)

Gaveston's paradise is attached to a person (the king) and not to the place or its population ("Not that I love the city or the men"). This qualification, dismissive as it is of the life of the city and its people, crucially degrades two of the stock notions that defined England's paradisaical qualities. Firstly, England styled itself as the inheritor of Troy's excellence, tracing its origins to the Trojan Brutus (from whose name, legend had it, "Britain" derived). London, as the metropolis of this new civilization, had been commonly referred to as Troynovant ("New Troy") at least from the thirteenth century, and most authoritatively in Caxton's *Chronycles of Englande* (sig. Biiii [*sic*], 4). Gaveston's inferred denigration of "the city" verges on mythical heresy. Secondly, the slur he casts on its inhabitants serves only to compound the insult. A land of great monarchs, true, but one built inexorably on the industry and courage of its subjects. The English paradise depended fundamentally on cooperation and internal peace between and within all social levels. Thomas Lodge in *The Wounds of Civil War* offers a salutary lesson on the need for universal social concord: "Brute beasts nill break the mutual law of love, / And birds affection will not violate; / The senseless trees have concord 'mongst themselves, / And stones agree in links of amity" (1.1.260–63). Without a land of harmonious subjects, there can be no peace—and peace was the essence of the English Elysium. Hal's cloaked foray among his ordinary soldiers on the eve of Agincourt in *Henry V* epitomized the tacit English communion between those who lead and those who are led. Albion's rare paradise could not be separated from the peoples who inhabited it, whatever their social standing or economic status.

As Gaveston elaborates on his notion of paradise on earth, it seems that the common people have no real part to play in his myth except as actors in a fantastical reverie:

Like sylvan nymphs my pages shall be clad;
My men, like satyrs grazing on the lawns,
Shall with their goat-feet dance an antic hay.
Sometime a lovely boy in Dian's shape . . .
Shall bathe him in a spring; and there, hard by,
One like Actaeon, peeping through the grove,
Shall by the angry goddess be transformed . . .

(1.1.57–60, 65–67)

There are many reasons why a period audience might have found this speech uncomfortable and, rightly, it has attracted sustained critical attention. David Bevington and James Shapiro have noted that Gaveston's "Italianate spectacle includes homoerotic fantasies of a 'lovelie boye in Dians shape'" (266). Lawrence Normand has drawn intriguing parallels between this scene and the sodomistic murder of Edward, suggesting that these two "utterly opposed versions of male same-sex eroticism frame the action of the play" (188). François Laroque has argued that "Actaeon's dogs represent servants turning on their master"—an interpretation that may have served "to adumbrate the barons' rebellion against their king" (169).

Gaveston's sense of paradisaical life in the English court is classically mythological but it is irreconcilable, even antithetical, to the sentiments of the nationalistic mythology that was so firmly rooted in the Elizabethan psyche. The lip service to paradise is there but the philosophical construct runs all awry. If we are looking for statements redolent of an English paradise, then it quickly becomes apparent that Gaveston is a bogus mythologizer whose image of paradise is far removed from the anglicized heroic ideal. His paradise is Arcadian, indulgent, personalized, private. And more than this, it is potentially destructive. William B. Kelly, though stopping short of labeling Gaveston as Machiavellian, has demonstrated how the "sylvan nymphs" speech may even challenge virtue in its broader sense: "The relish Gaveston displays as he details both his role in directing his men about their antics and the choreography itself is reminiscent of the delight in misdeeds associated with the morality play Vice figure" (10).

In the second scene of the play, another would-be mythmaker emerges, one who seems far more in tune with the precepts of the idyllic English mythology. Aggrieved at the return of Gaveston, several noblemen discuss with the Archbishop of Canterbury and Queen Isabella, Edward II's estranged wife, a possible course of action:

> CANTERBURY: But yet lift not your swords
>   against the King.
> LANCASTER: No, but we'll lift Gaveston from
>   hence.
> WARWICK: And war must be the means, or he'll
>   stay still.
> ISABELLA: Then let him stay; for, rather than my
>   lord
> Shall be oppressed by civil mutinies,
> I will endure a melancholy life,
> And let him frolic with his minion.
>
> (1.2.61–67)

cf. Homilies

Canterbury raises no objection to civil war and asks only that the king not be harmed; Lancaster promises force of arms to dislodge Gaveston; Warwick thinks of civil war as an imperative. Only Queen Isabella puts forward a contrary view, rejecting civil war utterly and proposing the sacrifice of her personal happiness for the good of the country. Her message is simple and unequivocal: death and destruction through civil war must be avoided. Peace must be maintained at any price. We could speculate, as some have done, that this is mere posturing—that she understands full well the inevitability of civil war and that her words are cheap—but at face value she affirms a central tenet of the English mythology: peace at home. The Elizabethan concern with civil strife was obsessive and a litany of sixteenth-century commentary reviles the idea of war on English soil. Among the most celebrated of these was Samuel Daniel's *The Civile Wares betweene the Howses of Lancaster and Yorke* in which the author sets out his stall very clearly in "The Epistle Dedicatorie":

his primary purpose is the need "to shewe the deformities of ciuile Dissension" (sig. A2ᵛ). And with good cause; the two hundred years preceding Elizabeth I's ascent to the throne had seen the bloodiest period of English civil history. The Battle of Bosworth Field (1485), the last great battle of the Wars of the Roses, bringing to an end a calamitous century of civil strife, would have been within living memory for a scattering of the early Elizabethans. It was frighteningly proximate.

In Elizabethan literatures, the curious composite of fighting spirit and peace-loving inclination was commonly characterized as a symbiotic relationship between the Roman god of war, Mars, and the prudent goddess Pallas. The anglicized cosmology is neatly summed up by Henry Peacham in *Minerva Britanna*. In an emblem titled "Quæ pondere maior" (44), Peacham reveals the hand of God extending from heaven and holding a set of scales (see fig. 8). In the left scale there is a cannon, in the right a bay leaf wreath and a quill. The accompanying verses read:

> BEHOLD a hand, extended from the sky;
> Doth steddilie a peized ballance hold,
> The dreadfull Cannon, in one scale doth ly,
> The Bay ith'other, with a pen of Gold;
> > Due to the Muse, and such as learned are,
> > The other Symbole, of th'art Militar.

> Though *MARS* defendes the kingdome with his
> > might,
> And braues abroad his foe, in glorious armes,
> Yet wiser *PALLAS* guides his arme aright,
> And best at home preuentes all future harmes:
> > Then pardon Soveraigne, if the pen and bay
> > My better part, the other down doe wey.

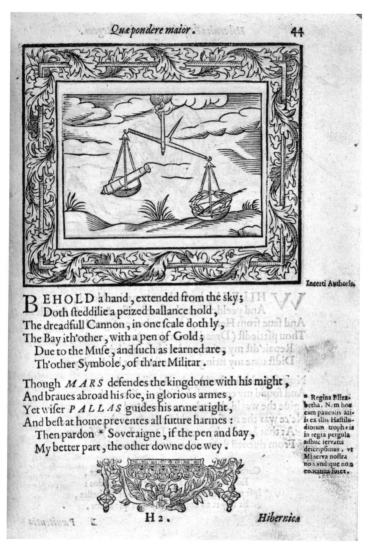

Figure 8. A woodcut titled "Quæ pondere maior" (What stronger thought) suggests that the pen is mightier than the cannon—or, framed in classical terms, the brutal zeal of Mars requires the sage counsel of Pallas. From Henry Peacham's *Minerva Britanna: Or A Garden of Heroycal Devices* (London: William Dight, 1612), 44. Reproduced with the kind permission of the University of Glasgow Library, Department of Special Collections.

This unique English deific relationship found currency in a range of popular literatures. Gerard Leigh in 1583 writes of the anglicized war god as Pallas's knight, "an armed Mars, A champion pollitique in fielde to fight, or at home to defende" (fol. 129ᵛ). William Wyrley, in *The Trve Vse of Armorie*, quotes a great English soldier as declaring: "For highly was my knightly seruice deemd, / As well for Mars as prudent Pallas grace" (135). English mythology claimed Mars as the protective god of England through the Trojan Brutus. On the authority of Geoffrey of Monmouth's *Historia Britonum*, looking upon the shores of Britain Julius Caesar declared that the Romans and the British had a common Trojan origin. According to Geoffrey of Monmouth's text, Caesar affirmed that Brutus founded Britain, just as Aeneas founded Rome (2).[3] And the patron deity of Rome was Mars. The role of Pallas in this English equation was clearly a later addendum but, with half an eye to the queen who ruled them, the Elizabethans clearly felt comfortable with the idea of brute masculinity moderated by feminine wisdom.

So Peacham's English Mars tutored by Pallas kept peace at home but abroad spurred the English to victory "in glorious armes." As she counsels the war-like barons against their zealous and bloody intent, Isabella offers the lone voice of reason. In urging the noblemen to pursue domestic peace, Isabella presents herself as a Pallas pleading for calm in the rush to war. That she should champion the civil peace of England might have puzzled Marlowe's audiences for she, too, was French. Yet who could prefer the violent solution proposed by Warwick to an existing peace, marred as it may be by the king's thoughtless and dissolute behavior? Isabella's position may well pose more of a conundrum for twenty-first century audiences, accustomed to the public accountability of those who govern, than it did for sixteenth-century audiences whose minds were so prodigiously scarred by Holinshed's *Chronicles* and other popular histories of the Wars of the Roses.[4]

Isabella's peaceful advocacy is therefore appropriate and had the king's fondness for Gaveston resulted in merely localized excesses her view might have prevailed. It is, indeed, part of Marlowe's skill as a dramatist that he can position someone like Isabella in a choric myth-validating role only to reveal within a short time new complexities that test the moral ground upon which characters and audience alike have positioned themselves. Within an act, the localized problem is suddenly internationalized. Lancaster and the younger Mortimer report to the king that England's peace is under foreign assault from four directions:

> LANCASTER: Look for rebellion; look to be
>   deposed.
> Thy garrisons are beaten out of France,
> And lame and poor lie groaning at the gates.
> The wild O'Neill, with swarms of Irish kerns,
> Lives uncontrolled within the English pale.
> Unto the walls of York the Scots made road,
> And unresisted drave away rich spoils.
> MORTIMER JUNIOR: The haughty Dane
>   commands the narrow seas,
> While in the harbour ride thy ships unrigged.
>   (2.2.160–68)

With peace at home destroyed by an invading Scottish army and foreign military reputation abroad compromised by the Irish, the French, and the Danes, the English myth is disintegrating before our eyes. This fact Isabella laments, wishing in 2.4 that "mine arms could close this isle about" (2.4.17). For the moment, though, matters are beyond maternal consolation. The greater imperative of England's safety against foreign foes nullifies Isabella's resistance and, whether she approves or not, the dissident noblemen begin their putsch with a move against the king's arch-flatterer and distracter, Gaveston.

Duly captured by his foes, Gaveston is loaded with all the crimes of an anti-mythologizer. It is he, young Mortimer curses, who has been the "proud disturber of thy country's peace" (2.5.9). Lancaster compares his crime to the unforgivable destruction of Troy caused by Helen, describing him as a "Monster of men" who "like the Greekish strumpet

[Helen of Troy]" has caused "so many valiant knights" to take the bloody field of (civil) war (2.5.14–16); and Warwick infers that Gaveston must die, not out of revenge but for "our country's cause" (2.5.22). Sara Munson Deats suggests that the Helen of Troy reference "indirectly connect[s] Edward with Paris, the passion-driven sybarite whose fatal amour led to the desolation of his country" ("Myth and Metamorphosis" 308). It is perhaps for this reason that Warwick insists that Gaveston will be brought to account not out of personal spite but for the good of the country. In sum, Gaveston is scandalized as the aggregate of all things that have led to the wane of England's heroic myth. His actions are compared to the very process that had destroyed that most civilized jewel of the English imagination, Troy itself.

With open conflict in Act 3, scene 2, and the ensuing execution of a string of English nobility, the country descends irresistibly into the brutal mire of civil war. Within a scene, Isabella, the one-time choric defender of the English myth for whom war on English soil had seemed anathema, has committed herself to the raising of French support for an army of invasion—a *French* army. And an act later, in a startling reversal of her earlier position, she suddenly turns her impassioned call for peace into an eloquent defense of the need for civil war:

ISABELLA: . . . a heavy case,
When force to force is knit, and sword and glaive
In civil broils make kin and countrymen
Slaughter themselves in others, and their sides
With their own weapons gored. But what's the help?
Misgoverned kings are cause of all this wrack,
And, Edward, thou art one among them all
Whose looseness hath betrayed thy land to spoil
And made the channels overflow with blood.
Of thine own people patron shouldst thou be,
But thou—

> MORTIMER JUNIOR: Nay, madam, if you be a
>   warrior,
> You must not grow so passionate in speeches.
>   (4.4.4–15)

It is a grave lament, and it reflects the dissolution of her commitment to Edward as her husband and as her divinely appointed king. The reversal of her position may be attributed partly to the belief that for the country to be peaceful once more it must now pass inevitably through the maelstrom of civil carnage. Perhaps she is right. Yet however fluently and sincerely it is couched, this is treason—a fact surely not lost on the young Prince Edward (soon to be Edward III) who stands, silent for the moment, by her side.

The dissident noblemen hardly need encouragement in the dash to war. They have already seemed quick, too quick, to draw their swords against English flesh. Among them, Mortimer stands as a vengeful icon—terse, impatient, uncompromisingly brutal. He is certainly reminiscent of the revenger god, Mars Ultor, described in Stephen Batman's *The Golden Booke of the Leaden Goddes* (1577), the sixteenth-century English vulgate of classical lore, who when he "inuadeth, all thinges are lefte desolate, & destroyed" (sig. 6ʳ). He is that Mars who Bel-Imperia in *The Spanish Tragedy* automatically associates with war: "where Mars reigneth, there must needs be war" (2.4.35). He is a Mars utterly alien to an English landscape, spurred by the bloodthirsty lust for civil carnage, and driven not by the anxiety to see his country's wounds healed but by vengeance founded on personal outrage. Mortimer's Martian impatience is mirrored in the abrupt way he interrupts the queen's speech, affirming his scant respect for words. This is no time to "grow so passionate in speeches," he rebukes, when the more pressing need is to "wreck . . . with the sword" (4.4.22) the unacceptable edifice of Edward's England. Passion should no longer be invested in the refined contemplation of English history or culture or greatness; passion is the fiery elixir of combat, blood, and death. No home-defending and foreign-conquering Mars here but, in its place, the classical beast, the very antithesis of the English Mars. England is in the grip of an anti-mythology, and one to which Isabella, who had once stood as the choric defender of the English mythology, has tendered a disturbing fealty.[5]

* * *

The importance of lineage is emphasized from the outset of the play. The thing that seems to irk the English barons most is what they see as the unwarranted promotion and patronage of Gaveston by the king. This is evidenced by the deprecatory terms "base" and "peasant" so often uttered in the first act to describe the Frenchman. Even the moderate and sanguine Kent balks at the titular aggrandizement of the king's favorite, arguing: "Brother, the least of these [titles] may well suffice / For one of greater birth than Gaveston" (1.1.157–58). Gaveston cannot slot into the monarchial English mythology partly because he is French but also because he lacks the noble pedigree to do so. When the king pleads "You that be noble born should pity him" (1.4.80) he tacitly acknowledges his lover's shortcomings in this regard—and, of course, his own through this somewhat naïve appeal to the compassion of his detractors. Somehow, as Mario DiGangi suggests, he seems to think the nobles may understand his favoritism towards Gaveston as "a species of friendship" (204). In this he is much mistaken. The noblemen find the low-birth of Gaveston highly threatening, perhaps because he presents them "with a kind of mirror image, exposing the ungrounded character of sovereign order" (McAdam 210). This seems to me an apposite observation. The England the noblemen knew and loved relied for its preservation and perpetuation on a chivalric understanding rather than on a written constitution. Even today England still has no written constitution. In the English encomium, it was understood that rank had its privileges but also its obligations, and that dynamic finds restatement by the rebel noblemen both with regard to their own actions and those of the king.

This is how young Mortimer articulates his lineal obligation as he plans to attack and conquer the king's castle at Tynemouth:

> This tattered ensign of my ancestors,
> Which swept the desert shore of that Dead Sea
> Whereof we got the name of Mortimer,
> Will I advance upon this castle walls
>   (2.3.21–24)

The tattered ensign, and the name "Mortimer" itself, become emblems of an inheritance that demands for its perpetuation the repetition of heroic deeds. Between them, they define young Mortimer's identity. As the Elizabethans looked back at medieval and earlier history from the informed vantage point of the late sixteenth century, the importance of this regenerating heroism was clear to them. In Shakespeare's *Henry V*, Canterbury and Ely respectively encourage the king to war against France by suggesting that to do so would be to repeat and thereby sustain the heroic reputation of the past:

> Stand for your own, unwind your bloody flag,
> Look back into your mighty ancestors;
> Go, my dread lord, to your great-grandsire's
>   [Edward III's] tomb,
> From whom you claim; invoke *his warlike spirit,*
>   (1.2.101–04, emphasis added.)

> Awake remembrance of these valiant dead,
> And with your puissant arm *renew their feats.*
>   (1.2.115–16, emphasis added.)

Hal's "great-grandsire" is young Prince Edward who assumes the English crown at the end of Marlowe's *Edward II*. The pattern of encyclical regal excellence with which the Elizabethans were most familiar was the journey from Edward III and the Black Prince to Henry V and the fields of Agincourt but the legend stretched further than that: to Edward I (nicknamed "Longshanks"), the most successful of the medieval monarchs, and back again to the talismanic myths of King Arthur and the Emperor Charlemagne. This great tradition of military heroism and conquest rested heavy on the Tudor psyche, and the willingness of Elizabethan *literati* to appeal to its authority suggests its glow had not in the least dimmed by the age of Marlowe and his contemporaries.

This military might was, though, a myth of repeating excellence in *foreign* lands. In the case of young Mortimer, the invocation of the spirit of his noble forebears, of the principle of regenerating heroism as a means of defying the physical processes of death, is somewhat misplaced. The crusader ensign, which graced battles waged by his ancestors against infidels in the Holy Land, here flies in rebellion against the rightful King of England. This diminution of the heroic myth is something that finds persistent, and increasingly ironic, restatement as the play progresses.

Quickly, the initial discourse of lineage in Act 1 turns from a denigration of Gaveston to a denigration of the king himself in Act 2.

> MORTIMER JUNIOR: When wert thou in the
>   field with banner spread?
> But once! And then thy soldiers marched like
>   players,
> With garish robes, not armour; and thyself,
> Bedaubed with gold, rode laughing at the rest,
> Nodding and shaking of thy spangled crest
> Where women's favours hung like labels down.
> LANCASTER: And thereof came it that the
>   fleering Scots,
> To England's high disgrace, had made this jig:
> "Maids of England, sore may you mourn,
> For your lemans you have lost at Bannocksbourn . . ."
>   (2.2.181–90)

Bevington and Shapiro demonstrate how what they call the "decay of ceremony" (here evidenced in Mortimer's disparaging comments about dress codes) is interpreted by the nobles as "an offense against the hierarchical structure upon which they depend no less than the king"

(268). Edward has failed to live up to the heroic ideal that his noblemen expect of him. The inappropriacy of dress betrays that wider shortcoming. First, he has failed to carry England's glories on foreign fields, reducing the business of war to an effeminate pantomime. And second, he has fallen short of the obligation to preserve England's peace at home, allowing the Scots to ride roughshod over the northern English counties, bringing "high disgrace" to England's reputation. Small wonder then that the rebellious nobles, having secured Gaveston's second exile, revile him as "base groom, robber of kings' renown!"—the pluralization of "kings" suggesting a generic failure of the encyclical pattern of kingly greatness.

Surprisingly, the king's supporters take a view not too dissimilar to that of the rebels. Spencer Junior appeals to the lineage of Edward II and laments that the king has not dealt with his opponents in the manner that true majesty demands. If he were the issue of Great Edward Longshanks, Spencer Jr. claims, he would not suffer the insolence of the barons in his own realm (3.1.10–15). And if the king properly regarded his "father's magnanimity" (line 16) and "the honour of [his] name" (line 17) he would not tolerate such behavior from his subjects. Spencer Jr. appeals not simply to the king's sense of decorum but to a sense of inherited majesty. Edward is not behaving as an English king should behave and, perhaps as a consequence, he is not being treated as an English king should be treated. Edward himself struggles to resurrect a heroic aura around himself but one of his difficulties, as Mitali R. Pati points out, is that his "myth-clichés block his perception of his real political situation" (164). Edward is adept at classical allusion, at constructing the resonances of a classical myth, but this process serves only to impinge on his ability to perceive problems of state and to resolve them realistically.

It is a delicious irony that Spencer, the herald of these hard heroic truths, has himself been precipitously promoted to greatness from the obscurity of peasanthood but, quite possibly, Marlowe does not intend us to read his comments as ironic. In England's socially stratified but all-encompassing mythology even the humblest of peasants understood the obligations of greatness. Spencer's words evidently sting Edward and just over a hundred lines later, when his foes are brought as prisoners before him, he falls to his knees and swears a fearful vengeance "By this right hand, and by my father's sword" (3.1.130). Rising to his feet again, Edward attempts to assume the mantle of Mars, the sometime defending deity of England:

> Treacherous Warwick, traitorous Mortimer!
> If I be England's King, in lakes of gore
> Your headless trunks, your bodies will I trail,
> That you may drink your fill and quaff in blood,
> And stain my royal standard with the same,
> That so my bloody colours may suggest
> Remembrance of revenge immortally
> On your accursèd traitorous progeny,
> You villains that have slain my Gaveston.
>
> (3.1.134–42)

In straining for a conception of military insuperability, Edward drifts away from the Pallas-tutored Mars of the emblem books and into a vacuous, self-centered rant—a further example of what Pati calls "the misuse of rhetoric" (163). With his talk of lakes of blood, draughts of blood, headless trunks, and unending revenge, he reminds us of the grotesque figure of Death in the palace of Mars offered in Richard Linche's truncated translation of Vincenzo Cartari's *Le imagini de i dei de gli antichi* (1556):

> wherevpon a stately altar, he [Death] was offering
> sacrifices in goblets made with the skuls of men, and
> filled vp euen to the brim with humane bloud; which
> oblation was consecrated to god Mars, with coales of
> fire (which set on flame the sacrifice) fetcht from
> many Citties, Townes and Holds, burnt and
> ruinated by tyrannie of the Warres.
>
> (sigs. XI^r–XI^v)

The rebels will be punished not for what they have done against England but for what they have done against Gaveston. Their blood will spatter the royal standard not as a warning against those who have ploughed up England's peace but as a "Remembrance of revenge immortally" (line 140). The death-defying lineage of regenerating heroism is transformed into a death-dealing lineage of regenerating regret, which will visit grief on the "accursed traitorous progeny" (line 141) of those who killed his lover. The mire of civil war has unleashed its monster—or at least that is how Edward erroneously would like to characterize his wrath—and there is no place for the learning and wisdom of Pallas. Edward imagines himself not as the English Mars dispensing justice and measured punishment with the greater good of the realm in the back of his mind but as the savage Mars Ultor intent only on blind, bloody retribution.

* * *

Claude J. Summers observes that because of "its failure to promulgate a political lesson compatible with Tudor orthodoxy," *Edward II* has been dismissed as a less than persuasive "history" play (222). Summers goes on to suggest that this omission is neither a flaw nor an irrelevancy since "the refusal to moralize history is at the heart of both the play's profound political heterodoxy and the personal tragedy of the king" (222). His views have found strong support, not least from Ian McAdam who sees the refusal to moralize as something that makes "the play more, not less, compelling as a work of art" (203).

Yet the present chapter argues that some degree of historical moralizing *is* going on in this play. The myth of heroic death-defying English excellence—of kingly son inheriting from kingly father, of civil harmony, of the anglicized construct of peace at home and glorious conquest abroad—is several times articulated by characters in *Edward II* only to be repudiated and degraded by ensuing circumstances. The competition between this mythology and what may be called its anti-mythology (the ignominious scenario of civil mayhem and English blood spilled by English hands) drives both the action of the play and the intellectual and emotional paradoxes that underpin it. With peaceful England lost, can only civil war reclaim it? Can anyone step forward to reclaim paradise? Gaveston's brief flirtation with the idea of paradise turns out to be spurious. Queen Isabella is ready and willing to state the precepts of the English mythology, presenting herself in the first four acts as a Pallas-type defender of England's peace, its native history of greatness, and the sovereign's untouchability. But her words and actions quickly disappoint. The young Mortimer and the king himself claim the mantle of Mars-like warrior, but in action and morality both fall short of the glorious ideal defined by Henry Peacham in *Minerva Britanna*.

In the final act Marlowe deftly steers us away from whatever vestigial sympathies we may have for the queen and the rebel cause. Her "moral metamorphosis" (Deats, "Myth and Metamorphosis" 313) complete, twice in the opening minutes of 5.2 Isabella encourages young Mortimer to murder King Edward, with the crude proviso that her name should be kept out of it; and the king's grotesque execution in 5.5 at the hands of Mortimer's emissaries leaves little emotional space aside from revulsion. By the time the youthful Prince Edward assumes the throne as Edward III the reputations of both Mortimer and Isabella have been sufficiently degraded to allow their punishments to stand as a sign of the new king's strength and decisiveness rather than as a continuing symptom of the indiscriminate depravity of civil malaise.

If Prince Edward's presence has been understated in the preceding drama, it is both dominant and kingly in the last scene of the play. Mortimer is summarily consigned to execution on the basis of hard evidence (his own letter); and Queen Isabella is committed to the Tower to await trial. At the end of *Edward II*, the newly crowned Edward III begins to demonstrate the true qualities of kingship—strength, justice, decisiveness. For this reason, Marlowe's subtitle to the play speaks of the "troublesome" reign and "lamentable" death of Edward II but stops short of describing the story as a tragedy. For the Elizabethan playgoer of the 1590s no saga that culminated in the coronation of Edward III could be defined persuasively as tragic. Nonetheless, there were important lessons to be taught and learned in the turbulent preamble to his coronation, and the personal travails and sufferings of Edward II relate directly to them. Edward's kingdom disintegrates not through calamitous and unusual circumstances but through what Patrick Ryan calls "entirely natural causes—human weakness, cruelty, and lust for power" (465). The resurging excellence of an English paradise, capable of renewing its greatness and thereby defeating the processes of physical death, relies on a precise concatenation of circumstances and dispositions. It is a delicate balance and one that can never be taken for granted. With Edward III on the throne a great phase of English history begins but Marlowe's play reminds its audience that England's natural seat of majesty is both glorious and vulnerable.

Notes

[1] Silvester Jourdan calls Bermuda "one of the sweetest Paradises that be vpon the earth" (sig. A3^r). Captain Bingham, in his prefatory poem to George Peckham's *A Trve Report, Of the late discoueries, and possession, taken in the right of the Crowne of Englande, of the New-found Landes*, describes Newfoundland as "The paradise, of all the world" (10). Thomas Stocker calls the Low Countries "the Paragone, or rather, yearthly Paradise, of all the Countries in Europe" (sig. A2^r).

[2] Josephine Waters Bennett has traced the origins of the legend of Britain as an isolated island paradise separated from the rest of the world and argued for "a more nebulous and vague association of Britain with the mythical islands of the Western Ocean, such as Thule, the Fortunate Isles, or Hesperides, the Islands of the Blest, and Homer's Ogygia" (117). Equations of England/Britain and Eden abound in late sixteenth-century English letters. Thomas Stocker frames his praise of England in biblical terms when he writes "For, where can wee read either in the olde Testament, or yet in any other prophane Historie, that euer *GOD*, dealte more bountifully, with any Nation then with us [the English], either for thynges needefull and necessarie, or delightfull and pleasaunt for this life.

So that it maie verie well be saied of us, that we enioye a lande, flowing with Milke and Honie" (sig. A2ᵛ). Robert Greene anticipates John of Gaunt's Second Eden motif in *The Spanish Masquerado*: "Seeing then we are euery way blest and fauoured from aboue: that the Lord our mercifull God maketh England like Eden, a second paradice: let us fear to offend him" (n.p.).

[3] G. H. Gerould, in his article "King Arthur and Politics," believes that Geoffrey issued his history between 1136 and 1138 (34).

[4] Holinshed's *Chronicles* were Marlowe's primary source for *Edward II*— see Maureen Godman, "Stow's *Summarie*: Source for Marlowe's *Edward II*."

[5] While few Elizabethans could have approved of her actions, there were numerous efforts in the Elizabethan period to analyze her support of the rebellion—see Carol Levin, "John Foxe and the Responsibilities of Queenship."

Chapter 5. Murder and Mayhem in *The Massacre at Paris*

Written towards the end of Marlowe's brief life, *The Massacre at Paris* offers a fast moving train of on-stage brutality, leading Andrew M. Kirk to style the play as the re-creation of French history "as a series of meaningless violent acts" (193). In its typical homicide, a victim pleads for life or time or both, and in each case death follows as certainly as it has been promised. Though a product of Marlowe's later career, the play seems to lack the introspective maturity and ideological complexity of *Doctor Faustus* or the *Tamburlaine* plays, both placed by the most recent scholarship within a few years of its composition (Burnett, *The Complete Plays* xii). But while both *Faustus* and *Tamburlaine* focus on the fates of individuals venturing into an uncharted and unprecedented wilderness, *The Massacre at Paris*, as I shall argue, seeks to animate dramatically a very familiar iconic template—the *danse macabre*. In its way, this undertaking may be as adventurous as attempting to articulate the forfeiture of a human soul or the illusory deification of mortality.

The *danse macabre* or dance of death was originally a fourteenth-century species of theater performed in churchyards in France and

too confident of this

Germany. Actors, representing the full spectrum of human life, from pauper to monarch, paraded before the audience with varying degrees of humility or vanity. In due course, Death figures dressed in black costumes with the human skeleton painted in yellow on their clothing would advance on the assembled host from nearby charnel houses, seizing each earthly representative in turn and dragging him or her off to the grave (Mâle 375–422; Ariès 18–23). Kings, queens, cardinals, bishops, merchants, mendicants, nuns, courtesans, tricksters, dancers, the old and the young, and many more—each in turn was grasped by the hand of jigging Death and led away. Though many would resist or argue or beg or cry for help, escape was impossible. On the journey to the grave, the Death figures would sometimes pause to scoff at a particular victim's worldly station or pretensions, reminding all present that mortality was the great leveler, favoring no one and sparing none.

By the sixteenth century the theatrical form of the *danse macabre* had largely disappeared, leaving behind two enduring legacies. The first was an explosion of artistic interest in the iconic image of cadaverous Death assailing living human beings. The celebrated 1424–1425 mural in the Charnier et Cimetière des Innocents in Paris, representing a series of vignettes from the *danse macabre* theater, inspired artists for the century and a half that followed (Clark, *The Dance of Death by Hans Holbein* 7–36). Though demolished in the seventeenth century the detail of the series was preserved in Guy Marchant's 1485 text *La danse macabre*, which ran to fourteen editions before 1500 (Herbrüggen 646). The Innocents series was also seen by an English monk, John Lydgate, who copied its images and translated its written commentaries. His work is known to have inspired *danse macabre* tableaux in various English church and cathedral settings, including the series in the cloister of Pardon Churchyard, near St. Paul's Cathedral, which according to John Stow was demolished in 1549 on the orders of the Duke of Somerset (Stow 310). Images of skeletal Death figures erupted on the walls and bosses of churches across Europe, in the margins of books and pamphlets, on the lids of snuffboxes and the handles of ale tankards, on the silver spoons of rich houses and the marble columns of priories. Much of this was no more than studious reproduction, but some of it was art of the highest order: as with the late medieval fresco in the Church of St. Mary at Beram in Croatia or the exquisite wood carvings in the misereres of the Drapers Chapel at Coventry Cathedral in the West Midlands, sadly destroyed by fire in 1940.

The second legacy, and one inextricably intertwined with the first, was the evolution of the *danse macabre* out of a mere species of theater and into a quasi-ecclesiastical scheme of human destiny. Medieval Catholic Europe, riddled with crime and war, and stalked by the specter of the Black Death, found in the figure of an animated cadaver a *topos*, a cultural icon, a social symbol that compassed at once both the certainty and mystery of the mortal condition. The physical surety of death was apparent everywhere; yet, for the individual, the moment of death was unknown, its territory incomprehensible, its advent a clarion call to terror. This conundrum is wonderfully illustrated in an illuminated German manuscript of the fifteenth century now held in the Warder Collection, New York: a priest baptizes a baby in a church font while a grinning cadaver stands at the ready with a towel in his hands (see Lerner, Meacham, and Burns 359). Death, the great leveler, was and is an insoluble enigma: his coming forever certain but the hour of his arrival unknown. These two streams of *danse macabre* inheritance—the artistic and the quasi-ecclesiastical—find perfect confluence in the work of the sixteenth-century Dutch emblematist Hans Holbein the Younger, whose *danse macabre* woodcuts with their weighty religious epigrams in *Imagines Mortis* combine an exquisite artistry with clear religious intention. *Imagines Mortis* was one of the most popular books of the sixteenth century, and especially so in England, since Holbein had been court painter to Henry VIII and is believed to have executed a dance of death mural in Whitehall Palace which was subsequently destroyed by fire in the seventeenth century.[1] Holbein's skeletal specter typically operates alone, grabbing or spearing victims when they least expect it and ignoring the occasional pleas for a moment's respite to pray or bid farewell to loved ones. "The Pedlar" (print xxxvii), for example, demonstrates the dynamic admirably: Death grasps a backpacked pedlar, who points to the road ahead, pleading, perhaps, for a short reprieve to put his earthly affairs in order. But the skeleton's antic grin and his trumpeting companion in the background affirm that the victim's time is up.

The Massacre at Paris is suffused by death. Death pervades every scene of the play from Catherine's menacing aside in the first minute of scene 1 to Navarre's promise of fatal revenge in the last seconds of scene 24. Could it be that in presenting the theatrical spectacle of zealous Catholic gangs roaming the streets of Paris searching out Huguenot victims, Marlowe is working in some way towards the visual and even psychological recreation on stage of a series of *danse macabre* vignettes? Is it conceivable that the cornering, the interrogation and the ruthless slaying of "heretical" Protestants is intended as a dramatic animation of one of medieval Catholic Europe's most recognizable and haunting *topoi*? If so, then *The Massacre at Paris* is surely a more complex theatrical construction than some have thought and Marlowe's purposes in writing it especially intriguing. It is difficult to deduce what kind of response the cultural and social associations of such a play might draw from its audience. Marlowe may have had in the mind the possibility of exploiting the partisanship of his Protestant playgoers but, with post-Armada London awash with anti-Catholic and anti-Papist propaganda, it seems unlikely that a man of his talent and intellect would waste time on the redundancy of yet another indignant diatribe. Possibly *The Massacre at Paris* was meant to cadence with its audience's sense of mortality and earthly transience but if that was its purpose what need was there to go to such extravagant and shocking lengths? The play's motivation may lie on different ground. Could it be a more universalized commentary on religious/political bigotry and on the delusional powers that bigots often presume for themselves—an ironic affirmation that Death is indeed the great leveler and that none, be he Catholic or Protestant, potentate or beggar, may claim its patronage or escape its grasp?

* * *

For much of its modern critical life, *The Massacre at Paris* was confidently categorized as anti-Catholic vitriol. Douglas Cole saw the Catholic enterprise as wholly evil from start to finish and John Ronald Glenn averred that "The Guise . . . is a purely Machiavellian figure" (373). More recent studies, though, have challenged the idea that an Elizabethan audience necessarily looked upon the play's bloody spectacle through simplistic anti-Catholic eyes—and have questioned as well the notion that the Guise is a figure of immitigable evil. Maryann Feola suggests that "woven into the drama of what was once discussed as anti-Catholic propaganda are threads which bind *The Massacre at Paris* to Marlowe's earlier work and his fascination with controversy" (7). Rick Bowers believes that "Marlowe presents terrorist violence and murder which, while officially criticized, also excites the very passions which it seeks to condemn" (131). He speculates that Marlowe "presents a mirror in which to stare with morbid fascination and a less-than-secure sense of English satisfaction" (139). Penny Roberts suggests that in death the Guise "appears more of the hero than the villain of earlier in the play" (435) and is "ennobled by a martyr's fate . . . whilst his murderer, Henry, appears sullied" (439). It was impossible, of course, for Marlowe to express any open admiration for the Guise but there seem to be suggestive ironies at work in the final scene of the play. The assassination of King Henry plays out against a background of misjudgment and fallibility. Henry's effusive praise for England and its queen is repeatedly undermined by his poverty of judgment, his ludicrous self-mythologization, and by the general moral treachery that pervades the play. The reasons for this may be connected to some political or psychological point that Marlowe was trying to make. Bowers suggests that in the Guise, Elizabethan's may have been encouraged to see a mirror of their own state: "the Guise obliterates opposition with the same efficiency as the Elizabethan regime" (136); Julia Briggs believes "the Elizabethan audience may have reacted to the violence [the slaying of the Huguenots] with excitement, as if they were watching real events, witnessing an execution or participating in a lynching, so that they laughed with the murderers, thus freeing themselves of responsibility and compassion, as the religious rioters themselves seem to have done" (278). *This would not please the authorities.*

Interpretations of *The Massacre at Paris* have been hampered by the presumption that it is, as Robert A. H. Smith puts it, "a shortened corrupt text" (496–97). W. W. Greg, introducing his edited version of the play, suggests that "even among admittedly garbled versions it has an evil distinction" (x). H. J. Oliver considered the work a text reproduced from memory (lii–lx); and Simon Shepherd attributes the play as much *in CD* to the invention of actors as of the author (xv). Kristen Elizabeth Poole has offered a full discussion of the play's textual origins (1–25). All this places the critic in something of a quandary since a reliance on words must be tenuous and the identification of systems of meaning necessarily circumspect. Indeed, in her admirable study of Marlowe's work, Sara Munson Deats excludes *The Massacre at Paris* from examination "on the basis that the corrupt nature of the play text renders any analysis—either ideological or formalist—highly suspect" (*Sex, Gender, and Desire* 20). While acknowledging these limitations of linguistic examination, I would argue that even if the precise wording of Marlowe's play has been lost to us there survives in the form of the drama and in the patterns of action something that may well be close to the spirit of what Marlowe intended. That form and patterning typically involve a series of brutal killings, often prefaced with humorous observations by the murderers and vain entreaties from the victims. Though we have trouble, as Penny Roberts has rightly observed, "in distinguishing [Marlowe's] words from those of the supposed reporter" (430) who wrote down the play from memory, the deathly stage spectacle itself may ring with more reliable authenticity.

The dance of death in medieval and Renaissance art is typified by a conjunction of humor and mindless, repetitive homicide. The skeletal emissaries of Holbein's prints are forever grinning and jigging as they lead off their victims. Even church renditions of the the skeletal form studiously preserve the antic disposition. In St. Alban's Cathedral in

Hertfordshire, for example, a monument to John Thomas Hylocomius features Latin verse written by former student John Westerman in praise of the learning and virtues of his old schoolmaster. Yet the accompanying mural shows not the image of a bearded academician clutching a book and exuding gravitas but, rather, a grinning skeleton in merry repose who has about him the distinct air of a naughty schoolboy. The humor works on two levels. First, the simple graphic looks like a piece of graffiti, doodled by a daydreaming pupil when the master's eyes were averted—a mischievous tribute to a much-loved teacher. But second, and perhaps more importantly, it reminds the viewer that despite the achievements of human life we, too, shall end up as "mere shades," to use Westerman's words. All of us shall be judged by our actions on earth and it is to be hoped that our case for heavenly reward will be as persuasive as that of the virtuous Mr. Hylocomius.

The dynamics of death in *The Massacre at Paris* appear similarly to mimic the humorous tenor of the *danse macabre*. Although Marlowe represents a massacre in an historic sense, as in the slaying of three thousand Huguenots in Paris on Saint Bartholomew's Day, August 1572, the dramatization of this event is effected through a series of caricatured killings, all richly textured with humor and irony.

> ADMIRAL: O, let me pray before I die!
> GONZAGO: Then pray unto our Lady; kiss this
>   cross.
>
> *Stabs him.*
>   (scene 5, 27–28)

> GUISE: Loreine, Loreine, follow Loreine! Sirrah,
> Are you a preacher of these heresies?
> LOREINE: I am a preacher of the word of God,
> And thou a traitor to thy soul and Him.
> GUISE: 'Dearly beloved brother'—thus 'tis written.
>   *He stabs him [and LOREINE dies].*
>   (scene 7, 1–5)

SEROUNE: O Christ, my Saviour!
MOUNTSORRELL: Christ, villain? Why dar'st thou to presume to call on Christ, without the intercession of some saint? *Sanctus Jacobus*, he was my saint; pray to him.
SEROUNE: O, let me pray unto my God.
MOUNTSORRELL: Then take this with you.
    Stabs him. Exit.
        (scene 8, 10–15)

GUISE: Why suffer you that peasant to declaim? Stab him, I say, and send him to his friends in hell.
ANJOU: Ne'er was there collier's son so full of pride.
    Kills [RAMUS, a Professor of Logic]
        (scene 9, 53–55)

GUISE: Come sirs,
I'll whip you to death with my poniard's point.
    He kills the SCHOOLMASTERS.
        (scene 9, 78–79)

Black humor is integral to each of these atrocities. Gonzago's "cross" is, of course, his sword which he uses both to deny his victim the time he seeks and to taunt his intention to pray. The Guise mocks the vocation of the preacher, Loreine, and taunts him with "an expression that would have been used in a contemporary Protestant service" (Burnett, *The Complete Plays* 573). In effect, Loreine perishes to the ironic echo of his own words. Mountsorrell's suggestion that Seroune use St. James as intercessor because "he was my saint" interposes a zany sliver of conviviality into the process of execution; the aristocratic Anjou, in dismissing Ramus's logical plea for mercy as an illustration of the sin of pride, cannot resist a wry swipe at the learned professor's humble origins; and the Guise seems to recall the corporal punishment of his boyhood when he promises a fatal revenge on the schoolmasters, vowing to "whip" them to death with his sword. This string of murders, occurring in successive scenes (scene 6 excepted but it is only three lines long), plays with an almost farcical freneticism on stage. Within the space of less than fifteen minutes an array of social representatives—an admiral, a preacher, a professor, a group of schoolteachers—is assailed, reviled, and executed. The murderers enter, kill, and exit with a mechanical repetitiveness, claiming absurd heresies for their victims and straining for a kind of crass, loutish wit in every death-dealing deed they perpetrate. It is as if the task of killing Protestants has become such a familiar avocation that its horrors have not simply been routinized into indifference but have actually become the source of mirth—rather like the gravediggers in Shakespeare's *Hamlet* or, indeed, the grinning skeletal emissaries in artistic renditions of the dance of death.

In the Elizabethan playgoer's mind, the iconic images created by these moments on stage would have resonated with a sheaf of emblematical images, ranging from woodcuts to church murals, in which humor and death colluded to make serious statements about the purpose and the destination of human life. In representations of the *danse macabre* it was common for skeletal figures to assume comically the demeanor and even the accoutrements of their victims. The 1554 edition of Lydgate's translation of Boccaccio's *The Fall of Princes. A Treatise excellent and compendious, shewing the falls of sundry most notable Princes and Princesses with other nobles* includes a woodcut of a *danse macabre* procession in which a skeleton has appropriated an ermined nobleman's staff of office and appears to be bantering with him. In Holbein's "The Abbot" (print xiv), Death wears the cleric's miter and bears his crosier over his shoulder (see fig. 9). A sixteenth-century memorial to Thomas Gooding in Norwich Cathedral reveals a smiling skeleton, his hands clasped in mock prayer, cheekily mimicking the clasped hands of the cathedral's living supplicants (see fig. 10). Similarly, Continental representations often present deathly emissaries anxious to parody those who have become their victims. Henri Knoblochtzer's medieval text, *Doten dantz mit figuren*, reveals a woodcut titled "La pucelle" (print xxxviii) in which Death, with a snake issuing

Figure 9. "The Abbot." Insolent Death, having appropriated an abbot's crosier and miter, unceremoniously drags him off to the grave. From Hans Holbein's *Imagines Mortis* (Lyon: Ioannes et Franciscus Fellonii, fratres, 1545), fol. A9ᵛ. Reproduced with the kind permission of the University of Glasgow Library, Department of Special Collections.

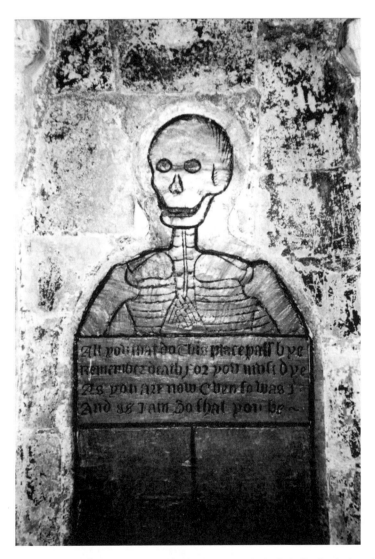

Figure 10. In this sixteenth-century mural from Norwich Cathedral, England, the pilgrim comes face to face with the skeletal image of one Thomas Gooding. The skeleton looks back at the viewer, his hands clasped in mock piety. Gooding's memorial stands as a warning to those whose spiritual posturing belies their earthly vanities.

from his mouth, dances absurdly with a distraught maiden. In a verse accompaniment, she admits to her faults: dancing and singing, not piety and prayers, have filled her time:

> J'ai voulu plaire au monde
> En dansant avec douceur ou vigueur
> Et aussi en chantant d'une voix suave.

Death's cavorting dance and the vile serpent slithering from his mouth serve to satirize the unwise abandon of the young lady's life, cautioning all observers to mend their ways before Death comes to ridicule *their* passing as well. The ceremonial of death expresses a clear link, albeit jagged and extravagant, between the earthly disposition of the victim and the physical behavior of her assailant.

These connections similarly exist in the serial murders of *The Massacre at Paris*. Intriguingly, the mood of the play is also lighter than its subject matter would give us cause to expect. Amidst the carnage and decimation, an audience regularly finds itself smiling, even laughing. Whatever serious purposes Marlowe had for *The Massacre at Paris*, he certainly intended the piece to be witty. This may be explained partly by the intrinsic humor of the *danse macabre*, which relies on an artistic sanitization of ritualized brutality—an experiential filter that intercedes between the gruesome detail of death and its artistic reproduction for an audience. Referring to a genocide from our own times, Glenn McNatt has described an official Khmer Rouge photograph he saw of a young girl whose life was purged in the charnel house years of modern Cambodia: "To gaze on the face of a 12-year-old victim is to be struck dumb by the horror that lies just outside the picture frame" (*Baltimore Sun* Internet Edition, July 27, 1997). We may be struck dumb but we are neither witnesses to nor victims of the nightmare. The full crime—its blood, gore, pain and unimaginable terror—is located beyond the work of art, outside the frame. Paradoxically, the photograph alerts us to a virtual monstrosity and yet intercedes to shield us from the full force of that monstrosity. We look upon the symbolic representation of the horror but not the horror

What about symbolic engagement w/ evil?

itself. As Marlowe's Protestant audiences sat fascinated by the artistic recreation of a Protestant holocaust, no doubt smiling (as we do today) at the verbal wit that most of the murders elicit, they must have felt more than a little uneasy—not so much because of the events of St. Bartholomew's Day, 1572, which might be dismissed as a localized insanity, but because in the eight years following the Paris massacre a Spanish army appeared to have institutionalized a program of Protestant genocide in the Low Countries. Herbert B. Rothschild, Jr., records that between 1572 and 1579

> . . . siege after siege of insurgent cities ended in
> atrocities. At Mechlin, Zutphen, Naarden,
> Oudwater, Sichem and Maestricht defenders and
> non-combatants were killed indiscriminately. The
> English were treated to a ghastly account of a sack
> when George Gascoigne published in London an
> eyewitness report of "The Spanish Fury" at Antwerp.
> (57)

No doubt, many Spanish veterans of the Dutch campaigns were aboard the Armada invasion force that was so fortuitously routed in the storms of 1588, less than five years before the first performance of *The Massacre at Paris*. It had been a close thing, though, and every English man and woman knew that only the grace of God had kept the Spanish killing machine from their shores.

As they watched the events of *The Massacre at Paris* unfold, none among an Elizabethan audience would have been unduly surprised by the Catholic propensity for extermination; and those who recognized the play's *danse macabre* motif might even have understood Marlowe's wry humor in placing in the hands of the Guise and his followers a script that had been written for them in the medieval churchyards of Catholic Europe. So, is this merely propaganda after all, using the vehicle of the dance of death to stir the deepest fears of Elizabethan England? Again, it seems unlikely. If *The Massacre at Paris* seeks to inflame religious

Appreciation

sensibilities by offering a salutary reminder of the genocidal antipathies of Continental Catholics, then what are we to make of the final scenes? The play's design may start with Catholic thugs searching out Protestant victims but it ends disobligingly with Protestant-inspired thugs hunting down Catholic victims.

* * *

The wanton brutality of *The Massacre at Paris* has perhaps played its part in making this the least popular of Marlowe's plays to modern sensibilities and has lent itself as evidence of his marginal authorship. Today, the play is hardly ever performed, and when attention does come its way, it is often reduced to a rehearsed reading. However, in late sixteenth-century London it was hugely popular. Kristen Elizabeth Poole, drawing on the earlier work of H. S. Bennett, points out that period records reveal the play's gate takings for 1593 were the highest of the season, suggesting that Marlowe's contemporaries valued the play far more assiduously than seems to be the case in our own times (Poole 4; Bennett 169). This may have been connected to the sense of insecurity Elizabethans felt across a whole range of issues, moving from the threat of foreign invasion to the possibility of a French marriage for their Queen. But it may also have had something to do with the way their society perceived and dealt with death. Though the superficial humor of the *danse macabre* may serve to carnivalize the moment of death, rendering it unpalatable to modern sensibilities, it would be wrong to think that such carnivalization diminished the serious import of that moment. We tend to shy away from a connection between humor and death. It is rare, indeed, that modern media infuses reports of death with mirth—to joke of death can so easily be misconstrued as an unseemly trivialization. But that is the etiquette of our own age, and the funerary mores of Marlowe's times were less reluctant to make such connections. On one level, we are surely meant to see the Guise, Gonzago, Mountsorrell, and others as butchers perversely rejoicing in their butchery. On another, Marlowe's audience may have recognized in the dramatic humor of assassination a mirroring of the *danse macabre*, in which the killers assume the role of Death himself bringing measured retribution, appropriately constructed and articulated, to those who have not loved their God. This association has the effect of creating a play within a play; a familiar pattern, abundantly alive in the visual art of Marlowe's day, working itself out in the dramatization of an historical tapestry.

No doubt, much of the play's early popularity lay in the discomfiture of what was perceived as Catholic pretentiousness and arrogance, an imperative that has lost its urgency in our own age. The willingness of the Catholic killers to self-mythologize themselves as Death itself is repeatedly confounded. Their assumption is rendered bogus on several levels—the would-be "Death" figures are fallible, whereas God's Death is infallible (the Admiral, for instance, survives the first attempt on his life); most of them are dead themselves by the end of the play; and no Elizabethan audience would have accepted for a moment the thesis that a murderous Catholic cabal could be acting at the behest of God. This last point is an important one. In medieval and Renaissance representations of the *danse macabre* it is understood, though not often stated, that the skeletal Death emissaries are commissioned by God himself. As evidence of religious *of Job* sanction, the genre was widely popular in church and cathedral settings. In England, where so much art was lost at the Reformation, the only surviving non-textual remnants of dance of death tableaux are all found in religious settings: in Hexham Abbey in Northumberland; in the Parish Church of St. Mary Magdalene at Newark-on-Trent; in St. George's Chapel at Windsor; and in the de la Warr Chantry at Boxgrove Priory, near Chichester in Sussex. There is also an interesting wall painting at Charlwood Church, Surrey, in the celebrated tradition of "The Three Living and the Three Dead," in which three rather static skeletal Death figures appear. Clark notes as well a dance of death series on the ribs of the choir vault at Rosslyn Church, near Edinburgh in Scotland (*The Dance of Chapel Death by Hans Holbein* 8). Emblematic representations of the *topos* are also common in the work of orthodox religious commentators of Marlowe's age. For example, John Daye's edition of Hugh Latimer's *Seven Sermons made vpon the Lordes Prayer* (1571) uses a dance of death image as its frontispiece. In mid-sixteenth-century theater, too, the image of skeletal Death was not uncommon, and the master–servant relationship between God and Death is wonderfully articulated early in the morality play *Everyman*:

> DETHE: Almyghty God, I am here at your wyll,
> Your commaundement to fulfyll.
> GOD: Go thou to euery man,
> And shewe hym, in my name,
> A pylgrymage he must on hym take,
> Whiche he in no wyse may escape.
> And that he brynge with hym a sure rekenynge
> Without delay or ony taryenge.
> DETHE: Lorde, I wyll in the worlde go renne ouer all
> And cruelly out-serche both grete and small.
> Euery man wyll I beset that lyueth beastly,
> Out of Goddes lawes, and dredeth not foly.
> He that loueth rychess I wyll stryke with my darte,
> His syght to blynde and fro heuen to departe—
> Excepte that almes be his good frende—
> In hell for to dwell, worlde without ende.
>
> (lines 64–79)

God's command is that Death should "shewe" those he seizes that they will be brought to "a sure rekenynge"; and Death affirms that he will "cruelly out-serche" the same, striking them with his dart. *Everyman* makes explicit the idea that Death plays an integral part in a divinely sanctioned scheme of crime and punishment.

Marlowe's audience would have understood well enough that the dance of death was a *memento mori* device, a relic from a less compromising religious age that weighed the ephemeral worthlessness of this world against the eternal treasure of heaven. The drama of *The Massacre at Paris* relies on this collective understanding for, without it, the subversive manipulation of its meaning would have been lost on the observer. In

Marlowe's perversion of the medieval schemata, the Guise himself appropriates the role of God, sending out his deadly agents not simply to kill people but to bring their "transgressions" to account. This blithe self-justification partly explains the antic demeanor of his emissaries; but it also speaks to the significant and overbearing sense of moral justification that finds expression before, during and after the killings. Just as in the typical *danse macabre* series there is no sense of compassion or consideration, merely of deserved retribution, so, too, those who kill the Huguenots seem void of restraint and remorse. The killings are styled as executions, commanded by the Guise and enacted without exception or moral compunction. If we are to believe the Guise, the recalcitrant impieties of the Huguenots have justified the terror of genocidal Death. As he spurs his henchmen to massacre the Protestants, five times he evokes the judgment of "heresy" to explain and justify their punishment (scenes 2, 4, 5 [twice], and 7). During the extended massacre the utterance of the term is his prerogative alone. Equally, he is adamant that none should be spared ("let none escape" he commands in scenes 6 and 7), his destructive impulse reflecting the extravagant distortion of a mind that has problematized a particular social group and can only envisage complete annihilation as the solution to that problem.

The Guise is a caricature of a human being, utterly beyond reason or argument, but it would be fanciful to suppose that he is a fiction of Marlowe's imagination, a demonic figment, for in our own times we have witnessed all too often the incomprehensible inhumanity of ethnic and racial cleansing. And in Marlowe's age, as we have seen, there was evidence enough of genocidal conduct on the part of Continental Catholicism—not least in George Gascoigne's contemporary eye-witness account of "The Spanish Fury" at Antwerp in 1576 in which more than eight thousand Protestant men, women, and children were slaughtered in the course of three harrowing nights. On the customary medieval moral edifice of the *danse macabre*, Marlowe builds complicated and contemporized Elizabethan significances—significances that remain unnervingly relevant to the concerns of our own times.

Self-deluded in his role as a God-figure, the Guise is as rudely surprised as his victims when the illusion of invincibility is finally dispelled. His own death follows the familiar pattern of wounding and moralizing. Warned that he is about to be murdered, he insists on his invulnerability, a claim ironically undermined by a classical self-mythologization. He trumpets his fearlessness, bandying his name about as if it is a talisman against the vagaries of the world:

> GUISE: Yet Caesar shall go forth.
> Let mean conceits and baser men fear death:
> Tut, they are peasants. I am Duke of Guise;
> And princes with their looks engender fear.
>
> (scene 21, 68–71)

These are grand, monumental words, the stuff of myth—the death-doomed myth of Julius Caesar. Does the Guise believe in his invulnerability or is this just another heroic template he suddenly requisitions to finesse the pathos of his death? What strikes an audience watching these moments on stage is his dislocation from the circumstances in which he has become fatally entangled. He is like a bad actor performing a hastily revised script rather than a victim reflecting bleakly on the last moments of his life. And to add to the absurdity, there is no audience on stage to witness his performance aside, of course, from the three murderers who stand poised to snatch his life. The Guise has become just another victim of the dance of death, at once brimming with declamation and vacuity and yet inevitably lost.

Mortally wounded, the process of his death begins predictably enough with the victim pleading for time to talk and with one of the assailants, bristling with righteous indignation, demanding that he seek forgiveness for his sins. This invitation the Guise declines, studiously replicating the typically unaccommodating pattern of the play's other victims:

> GUISE: O, I have my death's wound! Give me leave
> to speak.

> SECOND MURDERER: Then pray to God, and
>   ask forgiveness of the King.
> GUISE: Trouble me not, I ne'er offended him,
> Nor will I ask forgiveness of the King.
> O that I have not power to stay my life,
> Nor immortality to be revenged!
> To die by peasants, what a grief is this!
> (scene 21, 77–85)

The Guise is entirely unrepentant, still delusively at ease with the crimes he has committed and, by impugning the quality of his assassins, willing even at the moment of death to perpetuate the rhetoric of antic humor that he espoused as an assailant and now preserves as a victim. In the lines that follow, he clings steadfastly to the pagan comparison with Caesar whose own elevated pretensions were well-documented in Sir Thomas North's 1579 translation of Plutarch's *Lives* (60)—the same Roman parallel he had invoked in scene 2 to frame his over-reaching regal ambitions and, again, earlier in scene 21 to deprecate his foes.

> GUISE: Ah, Sixtus, be revenged upon the King.
> Philip and Parma, I am slain for you.
> Pope, excommunicate, Philip, depose
> The wicked branch of cursed Valois his line.
> *Vive la messe!* Perish Huguenots!
> Thus Caesar did go forth, and thus he died.
> *He dies.*
> (scene 21, 86–91)

He is a bogus mythologizer to the end, capturing his life in heroic antiquarian terms, conceding mortality more out of surprise than humility, and purporting to determine (as only God can) the moment of mortal death. He scrambles for words and grand images to construct an exit worthy of his self-image but instead slips comically into a mélange of vacuous comparisons and dissonant rant. And so the criminal conceits and unbridled arrogance of the Catholic cohort, their futile self-aggrandizements and theatricalizations, their preposterous moral claims and pathetic self-regard, are ground irredeemably into the Parisian dust. As a piece of Protestant propaganda, the play, up to this point at least, seems as dutifully biased as any man or woman in fin-de-siècle London could have hoped.

* * *

Yet, even as one bogus self-mythologizer dies, another dramatically steps forward to take his place. In the final scenes of *The Massacre at Paris*, Marlowe deliberately allows the political machinations of the play to slide out of control, to degenerate into an ever more absurd and ever less credible imitation of the medieval *danse macabre*. King Henry suddenly emerges from the Catholic camp, enlivened by a new-found anti-Papist agenda and effusive in his praise of Protestant England's queen, Elizabeth I. To give him even greater status, an English agent appears in the final scene of the play—his briefcase no doubt bulging with future possibilities for collaboration between the new France and Elizabethan England. Yet, for all this pomp and revised circumstance, the text studiously undermines Henry's judgment and monarchical credibility. He orders that the Guise's son should be brought forth to view the spectacle of his father's corpse—a notably ill-advised command since, within seconds, the boy has attempted to kill him. Styling himself as a death-dealer, Henry first claims to have killed the Guise personally ("twas I that slew him" [scene 21, 123]), immediately modifies the brag to suggest that those who did kill the king were simply his deathly proxies, and then, flourishing his new-found power and authority, dispatches his henchmen to kill Duke Dumaine and the Catholic Cardinal. To his mother, Catherine, the change in his demeanor is extravagant enough to make him unrecognizable: "Thou art a changeling, not my son" (scene 21, 149).

Within a few moments, two murderers are dragging the cardinal to his place of execution:

CARDINAL: Murder me not, I am a Cardinal.

FIRST MURDERER: Wert thou the Pope, thou
  mightst not 'scape from us.
CARDINAL: What, will you file your hands with
  churchmen's blood?
SECOND MURDERER: Shed your blood? O
  lord, no, for we intend to strangle you.
                                    (scene 22, 1–5)

Print ix in Holbein's dance of death series reveals "The Cardinal" assailed by grinning Death who snatches his hat from his head (see fig. 11). So, too, the new French court's murderous emissaries take pleasure in toying with their victim. Will they dare to shed a Catholic churchman's blood? No, is the jocular reply—they intend a *bloodless* execution. Summoning all the status he can muster, the cardinal attempts to assert his authority against Death but to no avail:

CARDINAL: Then there is no remedy but I must
  die?
FIRST MURDERER: No remedy; therefore
  prepare yourself.
CARDINAL: Yet lives my brother Duke Dumaine,
  and many more,
To revenge our deaths upon that cursed King,
Upon whose heart may all the Furies gripe,
And with their paws drench his black soul in hell!
FIRST MURDERER: Yours, my Lord Cardinal,
  you should have said.
                    Now they strangle him.
So, pluck amain; he is hard-hearted, therefore pull
with violence. Come, take him away.
                    Exeunt [with the body].
                                    (scene 22, 6–14)

Væ qui iustificatis impium pro muneribus,
& iustitiam iusti aufertis ab eo.

ESAIAE   V.

Væ nimium uobis qui iustificatis iniquum,
Erigitisq; malos, deprimitisq; bonos.
Donaq; sectantes fallacis inania mundi,
Iustitiæ uerum tollere uultis iter.

Figure 11. "The Cardinal." A cardinal is about to sell an indulgence to a supplicant bearing a chest of gold, unaware that Death is close enough to lift his hat. From Hans Holbein's *Imagines Mortis* (Lyon: Ioannes et Franciscus Fellonii, fratres, 1545), fol. A7ʳ. Reproduced with the kind permission of the University of Glasgow Library, Department of Special Collections.

Julia Briggs notes the similarity of this murder to those that have gone before: "The shedding of churchmen's blood had figured significantly in the massacre, where a similarly gruesome jocularity had accompanied the murders of the ministers [Loreine] . . . and Seroune. [Loreine], like the Cardinal, appeals in vain for clerical exemption" (268). But now, of course, Henry's anti-Papist murderers enact the ritual of the *danse macabre*, with a Catholic cardinal as their hapless victim. And even at the moment of death, one of the killers puns that the cardinal is "hard-hearted" and encourages his accomplice to pull harder on the rope (line 14). This final smear on the cardinal's character, suggesting his uncharitable spirit, echoes the biblical adage to Holbein's print, Isaiah 5:22–23, which berates those who have perverted the values of true piety. It also lends one further permutation to the multifarious possibilities of retribution. Dragged into the audience's view, the cardinal is strangled before our very eyes, and his lifeless body then unceremoniously carted off stage. It is shocking confirmation, if any were needed, that no mortal rank is less vulnerable than another to the varieties of death. In this play of poisoned gloves, musket wounds, stabbings, cuttings, stranglings, mutilations, and unending deviousness, no one is exempt from or immune to the barbarisms that man's ingenuity, in its state of postlapsarian wickedness, may conjure.

King Henry's self-promotion as the God-like commander of Death at the play's end is loaded with deliberate skepticism. He bears no more hope of moral rehabilitation than the Guise. In scene 24 he unwisely allows a friar into his presence without first having him searched. Then, while reading a letter, he is fatally stabbed. In this last phase of the play, King Henry, perhaps emboldened by the Guise's death, is suddenly driven to pass moral judgment on practically every foe who crosses or has crossed his path: the Guise is "Surcharged with guilt" (scene 21, 97) and will "sink away to hell" (98); the friar who has stabbed him will "feel in hell / Just torments for his treachery" (scene 24, 35–36). Yet, as he stands on stage, delivering verdicts like some deity or ministering angel, what presses hardest upon the audience's consciousness is his ultimate lack of power, his inability to control events or preserve even his own life. For all the grandeur of monarchy, his blood mingles on the floor with that of the beggar-friar who killed him. Elizabethan playgoers must have looked ruefully upon this sorry spectacle, for against it they surely tested their own misgivings about the aristocratic and religious rulers under whose control they lived and who sat not far from them in the more privileged stalls of the theater. The ludicrous sham of command accorded to the play's Catholic and Protestant ruling classes, rotten as it is with error and misadventure, suggests that the play's wider significance may extend beyond the realms of Continental holocaust and into the murky and muddled world of the governing Elizabethan elite.

As in Hans Holbein's image of "The King" (print viii) in the *Imagines Mortis* series, Death strikes at the very instant he is least expected (see fig. 12). Confounded and contorted with pain, Henry's final moments theatrically animate any number of *danse macabre* illustrations from the sixteenth-century emblem books. For all his majesty and anglophilia, it seems he has no greater claim to life than the Guise, the Huguenots, the Catholics or, indeed, the friar who ended his life. This is the quintessential lesson of the *danse macabre* but *The Massacre at Paris* is more than a simple imitation of a *memento mori* device; it is a subtle political and social interrogation. The denouement of the play, with its hollow moralities and cankered triumphalism, elicits from the audience a violent frisson of terror and self-reflection. In demeaning the judgment and values of a monarch who praises Eliza, and then ruthlessly slaying him, Marlowe invites his audience to consider the emotional manipulation that his theater has wrought upon them, to recognize that what they had presumed was anti-Catholic propaganda has somehow reshaped itself into moral irony and painful introspection. The English agent who stands silent in the bloody miasma of scene 24 watching in horror as the French king's life passes away is in some part an ordinary mortal reviewing the transience of human life. In another guise he is England itself witnessing what happens to a nation whose ruling class is captivated by earthly vanities and the mindless determination to obliterate any world view that runs contrary to its own.

Figure 12. "The King." A king seems unaware of Death's approach. His earthly pomp and ostentatious wealth, evident in his clothing and treasure, now amount to nothing. From Hans Holbein's *Imagines Mortis* (Lyon: Ioannes et Franciscus Fellonii, fratres, 1545), fol. A6ᵛ. Reproduced with the kind permission of the University of Glasgow Library, Department of Special Collections.

Notes

[1] Holbein's most influential text was *Les Simulachres & Historiees faces de la Mort, avtant elegammet pourtraictes, que artificiellement imaginées* (1538). The book was renamed *Imagines Mortis* for the 1542 edition, and had been greatly expanded by the time Marlowe was born in 1564. Arthur B. Chamberlain in *Hans Holbein The Younger* lists some of the many editions of the *Imagines Mortis* that appeared in various parts of Europe in the sixteenth century (212–14). After the first edition in 1538, ten further (and progressively enlarged) editions followed over the next twenty-four years. At the time of Marlowe's death in 1593, quite aside from the numerous official versions of the work, scores of pirated editions were in circulation across Europe, five of them appearing in Cologne alone, for example, in the twenty years from 1555 (Clark, *The Dance of Death by Hans Holbein* 32).

Chapter 6. Faustus's Contract and the Manipulation of Visual Resonances in *Doctor Faustus*

In the Prologue to *Doctor Faustus*, the Chorus announces to the audience that "We must perform / The form of Faustus' fortunes, good or bad" (7–8). The Chorus goes on to note the protagonist's unremarkable birth, his rise to doctoral excellence at Wittenberg and his fall from grace when "glutted more with learning's golden gifts, / He surfeits upon cursèd necromancy" (24–25). That this story "must" be performed suggests, perhaps, both the sense of obligation and the sense of reluctance that the Chorus feels. Georgia Brown's admirable study *Redefining Elizabethan Literature* demonstrates that shame obsessively presented itself as both a literary theme and a quite conscious authorial position in a range of fragmentary and marginal forms of expression during the 1590s. The opening of *Doctor Faustus* may be impelled by a similar preoccupation: the Chorus undertakes to present an unpalatable story—a shameful tale—but one that must, for the greater good, be told. If the Chorus is to be believed, the play is, in some important sense, a moral discourse and there is something to be *learned* from the story of Faustus.

The sense of moral instruction is pre-eminent, as well, in that most successful of sixteenth-century genres, the emblem book. A tripartite mix of motto, picture, and verse explication, emblem books approached their English acme in the golden age of Elizabeth I's reign. In some ways, *Doctor Faustus* is very much like an emblem book. Latin marginalia offering classical sources and commentary were popular in emblem books, evidencing the wide audience that the genre could command—from the illiterate who could satisfy themselves with the detail of pictures to the erudite who could read and write in several languages. Marlowe's play is characterized by a similar multi-leveling. We are invited to enjoy the visual rough and tumble of Rafe and Robin and Wagner but also to smile wryly (if our learning so allows) at their mangled Latin epithets. And Faustus's over-reaching ambition, evident to all, is often conjoined with and subverted by more subtle commentaries delivered through Latin syllogisms and classical or biblical allusions which are aimed at a much narrower audience.

There is similarity, too, in the succession of vignettes, often unconnected, that the emblem book offered its reader. The glorious swirl of Marlowe's story carries us from Wittenberg to Rome to the Court of the Holy Roman Emperor to (in a figurative or, if we believe Mephistopheles, a literal sense) Hell itself and back to Wittenberg, offering us glimpses of Alexander the Great and Roxana, Helen of Troy, a surrogate Actaeon, Darius, the rivals Pope Adrian and Pope Bruno, Satan, Lucifer, the Seven Deadly Sins, good angels, bad angels. The parade of exotic vignettes is reminiscent of the wide-ranging and disparate interests of the emblem books which typically flit from one morally edifying image to the next. For example, if we look to the religious and historical landscape of Geffrey Whitney's *A Choice of Emblemes* (1586), the most famous of the sixteenth-century English emblem books, we find a familiar population: the Deadly Sins (4, 31, 76), Diana and Actaeon (15), Helen of Troy (79), Lucifer (86), Alexander the Great (131), Satan (166), Fortune (181).

This is not to suggest that the playwright was consciously or even unconsciously attempting to produce a theatrical emblem book—the power and coherence of the Faustus story moves far beyond that—but it does seem to me that, at times, he may be deliberately exploiting the pre-knowledge of his audience with regard to emblem book techniques and structuring. He is, if you will, inviting the audience to bring their emblem book skills to the theater and to dissect and illuminate the theatrical emblems he creates for their entertainment. There are many illustrations of this. For example, when Helen of Troy appears on stage with Faustus fawning lasciviously at her heels in 5.1, did Marlowe expect his audience to make connections with their common reservoir of popular visual associations? In our own age, Helen of Troy, with her face that launched a thousand ships, is taken as an icon of tragic beauty. In song and word our contemporary culture has typified her as the incarnation of a certain purity of form. Faustus holds a similar view:

> FAUSTUS: Gentlemen, for that I know your
> friendship is unfeigned, and Faustus' custom is
> not to deny the just requests of those that wish
> him well, you shall behold that peerless dame of
> Greece, no otherways for pomp and majesty than
> when Sir Paris crossed the seas with her and
> brought the spoils to rich Dardania. Be silent
> then, for danger is in words.
> *Music sounds and* HELEN *passeth over the stage.*
> SECOND SCHOLAR: Too simple is my wit to
> tell her praise
> Whom all the world admires for majesty.
> THIRD SCHOLAR: No marvel though the angry
> Greeks pursued
> With ten years' war the rape of such a queen,
> Whose heavenly beauty passeth all compare.

FIRST SCHOLAR: Since we have seen the pride
   of nature's works,
And only paragon of excellence,

Enter an OLD MAN

Let us depart; and for this glorious deed
Happy and blest be Faustus evermore.

(5.1.17–32)

This is a remarkable exchange between Faustus and his like-minded friends. In prose, Faustus warns them to be "silent then, for danger is in words" (22–23), drawing that distinction between word and image that was the very epitome of the emblem books—and marking, as well, the divide between the intellect and the senses. The danger of words is, on the surface, the worry that any sound might frighten Helen away but it is also the fear that the interpretation of words may compete with the significance of image.

Faustus's first judgment of Helen is that she is the "peerless dame of Greece" (20). And, once she has passed over the stage, his friends agree. The Second Scholar confirms that she is someone "Whom all the world admires for majesty" (25); the Third revels in her beauty, little wondering that the "the rape of such a queen" resulted in ten years of war; and the First Scholar calls her the "pride of nature's works" (29) and the "only paragon of excellence" (30). High praise indeed and interesting, too, that once Helen has passed over the stage, the witnesses recollect her virtues in verse, that most elevated of literary forms, not in the prose style Faustus and his friends had adopted before her arrival.

The problem is that in Marlowe's age Helen's name carried with it the full weight of sexual impropriety and national disaster. As anyone who knew the emblem books would affirm, the verse gloss on the image of Helen in 5.1. does not provide an appropriate explication. The emblem books sometimes note Helen's beauty but, almost without exception, bewail the destruction that her beauty caused and revile the untempered carnal desires that brought her to Troy. Often the focus is more on the error of Paris than on the beauteous bedevilment of Helen, as in Geffrey

Whitney's interpretation: "Though PARIS, had his HELEN at his will, / Thinke how his facte [*sic*], was ILIONS foule deface" (79). We see similar images of Paris and Helen, with the same generalized moral implication, appearing throughout the sixteenth century—in Alciati, Marquale, Lefèvre, Daza, Hunger, de Bry.

This pejorative spin on the emblematic image is entirely lacking in the theatricalization of Helen and Paris (aka Faustus) in 5.1. Yet it surely could not have been far away from an Elizabethan audience's thoughts, and the Old Man who enters at the very height of the First Scholar's praise soon presents himself as a moral sentinel whose function seems to be to wrench the image back to the familiar moral ground of the emblem books. Like the emblem books, he focuses on the man, not the woman, and immediately chastises Faustus, speaking of:

> . . . thy most vile and loathsome filthiness,
> The stench whereof corrupts the inward soul
> With such flagitious crimes of heinous sins
> As no commiseration may expel
> But mercy, Faustus, of thy Saviour sweet,
> Whose blood alone must wash away thy guilt.
>
> (5.1.40–45)

So mortified is Faustus that he contemplates suicide and prepares to stab himself. But the grace of God, not suicide, is the answer the Old Man affirms (5.1.52–55) and Faustus pulls back to reflect on this. The Old Man exits and within a few lines Mephistopheles reappears, spouting crude threats, and cowing the once "resolute" Faustus into obeisance. When Faustus exits with Helen, thirty lines later, apparently to satisfy his low carnal instincts, disapproval of his action must surely have gathered an unstoppable momentum from its association with populist images such as that in *A Choice of Emblemes*. The folly of Paris is the folly of Faustus—a preoccupation with the present satisfaction at the expense of future joys. The Old Man reappears to assert a familiar message:

> Accursèd Faustus, miserable man,

> That from thy soul exclud'st the grace of heaven,
> And fliest the throne of His tribunal seat.
>   (5.1.109–11)

Another example. The fable of Diana and Actaeon, no doubt well known to all in Marlowe's audience, is presented in the manner of the emblem books—not as a simple account of an interesting classical story but as a modern narrative detailing another dimension of human folly. In the myth of antiquity, the hunter Actaeon inadvertently sees Diana naked and she, enraged, turns him into a stag. Pursued by his own pack of dogs, he is cornered and torn to pieces (see fig. 13). The emblem books, though, transformed the Actaeon myth into an account of moral debilitation and just punishment. Actaeon becomes a symbol of spiritual ugliness, driven by animal desires and carnal excess, whose annihilation is both inevitable and warranted:

> By which is ment, That those whoe do pursue
> Theire fancies fonde, and things vnlawfull craue,
> Like brutishe beastes appeare vnto the viewe
>   (Whitney 15)

It is difficult to see how the horning of the impudent Knight in 4.1 connects to emblematic interpretations of the myth. As far as we know, he isn't guilty of animal desires or carnal excess. He is horned at 4.1.77 because Faustus is peeved by his churlish skepticism. His humiliation is a very public humiliation, as Whitney suggests it should be ("appeare vnto the viewe"), but it is neither appropriate nor deserved. Did Marlowe expect that his audience's emblematic pre-knowledge might just have turned the image on Faustus himself—morally transforming *him* into the brutish Actaeon figure who has "things vnlawfull craue[d]"? The Knight is quick to call him a "damnèd wretch" who was "Bred in the concave of some monstrous rock" (4.1.81–82) and, within a few minutes of the horning caper, the Old Man is referring to Faustus's "most vile and loathsome filthiness" (5.1.40). And certainly, later in the same scene Faustus enjoys the kind of wish-fulfillment that

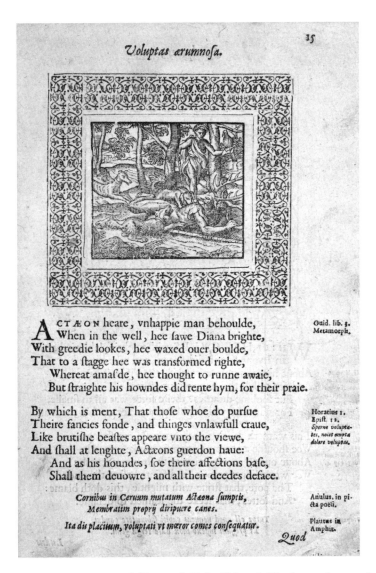

Figure 13. "Voluptas Ærumnosa" (Pleasure Is Full of Misery). The hunter Actaeon, having glimpsed Diana naked, is turned into a stag and torn apart by his own hounds in a woodcut from Geffrey Whitney's *A Choice of Emblemes* (Leyden: Christopher Plantin, 1586), 15. Diana observes his fate without any apparent remorse. Reproduced with the kind permission of the University of Glasgow Library, Department of Special Collections.

Actaeonesque voyeurs can only dream about. Having glimpsed Helen cross
the stage at 5.1.23 he "crave[s]" (5.1.80) of Mephistopheles her return so
that he may satisfy his lust "In wanton Arethusa's azured arms" (5.1.107).
This moment has both fascinated and troubled critics. David C. Webb sees
it as the cipher of Faustus's damnation, arguing that he "commits the sin of
demoniality, that is sexual intercourse with demons, and is damned from
that moment" (31). Others, like William M. Hamlin, have viewed it rather
as the consequence of earlier events and comments in the play.[1]

It is one thing to speculate about emblematic allusions but quite
another to say how or why a dramatist is using them. In the nineteenth
century Henry Green documented many hundreds of possible emblematic
allusions in Shakespeare's work but the great majority reflect nothing more
than the simple jingle and jargon of the age. The difficulty is always that
because the Elizabethans, like most Europeans, expressed their enthusiasm
for the Renaissance through promiscuous reference to the stories and
details of antiquity, weighing the wider importance of a given reference
isn't always easy. Shakespeare's *Henry VI* plays are a good illustration of the
unbridled willingness to "allude" which had become fashionable from the
1580s onwards, a willingness that was tempered only by the new and
darker desires of the Jacobean age.

In the case of *Doctor Faustus*, though, young Marlowe may well be
moving with greater purpose than young Shakespeare in the First
Tetralogy. While the examples I have cited so far reach to the heart of
some issues of the play, the emblems in question are not themselves
developed in a coherent way in the full process of the drama. Helen and
Actaeon may comment appositely on Faustus's misjudgments but as
images they are contributive rather than sustained.

*   *   *

I believe there is a more sustained emblematic development in the idea of
Fortune, which provided some of the most important iconic images of
the Renaissance. Fortune is intimately connected with Faustus's signing
of the contract with the devil in 2.1, an act that serves as the focal point

for a flurry of emblematic associations. In the remainder of this chapter I'd like to explore how Marlowe manipulates them and what his purposes may be in doing so.

From the start of the play everything builds towards the signing of the deed of gift in 2.1. Faustus is a scholar, and a scholar in many disciplines, and above all he values the power of the mind to harness and order the world around him. He thinks about words, uses them carefully, dwells on them. When Valdes urges him to be "resolute" about his ambitions, the word sticks in his mind. Twice in the minutes that follow he returns to it, as if it is a key in his pocket that he keeps turning over and over again. But by being resolute in his ambitions, Faustus inextricably connects himself not to learning, but to fortune. Visually, this idea had presented itself in the popular sixteenth-century image of Fortune counterpoised against Knowledge. The battle is beautifully illustrated in the frontispiece of Robert Record's *The Castle of Knowledge* (1556), one of the most important astronomical treatises of the sixteenth century (see fig. 14). Here, the astronomer's muse Urania ("whose gouernour is Knowledge") is pitted against the blindfolded Goddess Fortuna ("whose ruler is Ignoraunce"). In the centre of the picture, the Castle of Knowledge reaches high into the stars. To its left, Urania grasps a set of compasses (the epitome of scientific certainty) and holds also a sphere of destiny. She is calm and secure, standing on a solid stone cube. To the right of the castle, Lady Fortuna stands bare-footed and precarious on a ball. She is blindfolded, her appearance feckless and disheveled. Between her fingers, she holds a string that is attached to a wheel of fortune. A verse *subscriptio* reminds the observer that "The heauens to fortune are not thralle."

Record's woodcut, a Renaissance reworking of traditional images of Fortuna and Sapientia, was not original. Charles de Bovelles's 1510 cut of "Fortvna et Sapientia" (fol. 118ᵛ) had presented a blindfolded Fortuna seated on an unstable ball with Sapientia opposite, sitting on a solid cube and looking with admirable self-reflection into a mirror. The observer is invited to weigh the blind enthusiasm of Fortuna against the measured

Figure 14. "The Castle of Knowledge." The frontispiece of Robert Record's *The Castle of Knowledge* (London: R. Wolfe, 1556) revealing an image of Lady Fortuna. The Wheel of Fortune is placed in direct opposition to God's "Sphere of Destinye" and, as the verse epigram at the bottom of the page explains, proves no match for it. Reproduced with the kind permission of the University of Glasgow Library, Department of Special Collections.

judgment of Sapientia. In Symbol XI of Achille Bocchi's *Symbolicarum Quaestionum* (1555) Knowledge again looks into a mirror, emphasizing the awareness of self so lacking in the foolhardy zeal of Fortuna.

It is one of the play's early curiosities that a man steeped in knowledge and learning, as Faustus is, finds himself suddenly connected to the idea of Fortune. His natural choice should surely have been learning, and perhaps it has been thus far, but in this new phase of his learning—the phase documented in the play—his allegiance apparently shifts. As we have seen, the Chorus suggests as much in the first lines of the play when it promises to reveal the "fortunes, good or bad" of Dr. Faustus, and goes on later to explain the nature of Faustus's transgression:

> For, falling to a devilish exercise,
> And glutted more with learning's golden gifts,
> He surfeits upon cursèd necromancy.
> ("Prologue" 23–25)

The censorial, edifying tone is obvious, and reminiscent again of the emblem books. And it is similarly couched in the immediacy of the present tense, the Chorus concluding its introduction with the line "And this the man that in his study sits" (28). This presentism is characteristic of the emblem books where images of past events are typically contextualized in moral apothegms written in the present tense. The purpose is to remind the reader that these are lessons designed for temporal instruction and not merely entertaining anecdotes from days gone by.

From all of this we may glean further evidence of the familiar tenor of shrill morality that we find in the emblem books, the same sense of edifying spectacle and grim-faced warning. But there may be something else too. Though the Chorus speaks of fortune and speaks of knowledge, it doesn't connect them in the way the emblem books do. Marlowe's Chorus sees excessive knowledge as the cause of misfortune: "glutted more with learning's golden gifts, / He surfeits upon cursèd necromancy" ("Prologue" 24–25). The authority of the emblem books, on the other hand, views ignorance as the cause of misfortune. This disjunction would have jarred contemporary sensibilities and Marlowe appears to be throwing down an intellectual gauntlet to his audience: here is the Chorus's initial construction of Faustus's fall but will it be sustained in the action that follows?

When, in Act 1, scene 1, Faustus determines to unwrap the secrets of necromancy his objectives in so doing are almost laudable. There is, of course, a desire for personal power but there is also a promise of worthy undertakings—ranging from bright new clothes for young students to stupendous public works such as ringing Germany with a brass wall and diverting the Rhine to form a defensive moat around Wittenberg. His friends, Valdes and Cornelius, support his ambitions. Valdes imagines that their feats together will be such to "make all nations to canonise us" (1.1.122) and he urges "learned Faustus [to] be resolute" (line 135). Cornelius, too, applauds the ambitions of Faustus, viewing them as an intellectual "study" (line 139) and clearly envisaging his colleague's intentions as an exercise in scholarly learning (lines 140–45). Once more, the journey into necromancy is seen as a journey into knowledge.

Having summoned the devil, Faustus advances a daring proposal. He offers the devil a contract in which he is willing to surrender his soul in return for twenty-four years of necromantic ecstasy. When Mephistopheles returns, affirming that Satan is interested, he demands that Faustus signs a deed of gift with his own blood. The gift is Faustus's soul. A deed of gift is not necessarily a contract—it is a gift, typically used to apportion possessions to relatives and friends unconditionally after death. For a long time we wonder whether Faustus will fall into the trap not only of surrendering his soul but of surrendering it for nothing. However, when he unveils the deed he shows himself cleverer than we had feared. He attaches conditions to the deed of gift which effectively turn it into a contract. But having dodged one pitfall, Faustus inadvertently steps into another. The deed he writes in his own blood makes no mention of knowledge. His demands of the receiving party—his consideration, in legal terms—amount to a short and fairly contained list of requirements: the qualities of a spirit; Mephistopheles to be his servant; invisibility in his chamber or house; and the ability to appear in different shapes or forms. Nowhere is there a mention of knowledge.

William Tate suggests (incorrectly, I believe) that "After signing away his soul, Faustus's first demand of Mephistopheles is 'let me have a wife'" (4). This is perhaps his first "tangible" demand but it is surely not his *first* demand. The very minute he has signed the deed, Faustus demands knowledge from the Devil.

> FAUSTUS: [*Handing over the deed*] Ay, take, it, and
> the devil give thee good on't.
> MEPHISTOPHELES: Now, Faustus, ask what
> thou wilt.
> FAUSTUS: First will I question with thee about
> hell.
> Tell me, where is the place that men call hell?
> MEPHISTOPHELES: Under the heavens.
> FAUSTUS: Ay, but where about?
> MEPHISTOPHELES: Within the bowels of these
> elements,
> Where we are tortured and remain forever.
> (2.1.115–22)

To these questions of fact, Faustus receives no satisfactory answer, and the pattern of obfuscation and prevarication that Mephistopheles initiates here weaves its way through many of the exchanges with his victim—a point reiterated by numerous critics, among them L. L. James (30) and Pompa Banerjee (227–28). To this view, there are some dissenting voices. Jürgen Pieters, for example, has suggested that "As the play proceeds, it becomes ever clearer that this newfound knowledge will enable Faustus to do whatever his heart desires" (109). Pieters may be correct in suggesting that Faustus can mostly do what he wants to do after signing the contract. It is not newfound knowledge that grants him this gift but, rather, the agency of Mephistopheles. After signing the deed, truth be told there is very little newfound knowledge on offer to Faustus, and this is the moot point. The deed only places upon Mephistopheles the obligation to be Faustus's servant, not his tutor. In a precipitate and reckless drafting of his contract with Lucifer, and despite all the benign intentions of Act 1, Faustus has, in a quite extraordinary oversight, left out what seems to be the most important term of all—the acquisition of knowledge.

At the end of the play, indeed in the final sentence of the play, the Chorus returns to reiterate the fortune motif. The "fiendful fortune" of Faustus has led to his "hellish fall." The lesson is plain for all to see:

> Whose fiendful fortune may exhort the wise,
> Only to wonder at unlawful things,
> Whose deepness doth entice such forward wits,
> To practise more than heavenly power permits.
>
> ("The Epilogue" 5–8)

The words of the Chorus ring with the epigrammatic tenor of the emblem books: you "forward wits" in the audience with ambitions of necromancy—think again! The "wit" of Elizabethan usage was a seeker of knowledge, an intellectual, but there are limits to the legality of learning. Faustus, the Chorus affirms, has been one of those intellectuals whose thirst for knowledge has crossed legal boundaries. The pact with the devil has rendered little of worth. As the hour of his death approaches, he turns on the world of learning and bitterly rejects it:

> . . . I have been a student here these thirty
> years, O would I had never seen Wittenberg, never
> read book!
>
> (5.2.19–21)

This failure of knowledge is intriguing. Faustus laments learning and, indirectly, celebrates ignorance. The paradigm of an heroic intellectual rise to fame, so studiously chronicled in the Chorus's opening lines, is here utterly discredited.

The conclusion of the Chorus and Faustus could not be further removed from the moral adjudications of Record, Bocchi, and the other emblematists. For the emblematists it was knowledge that forestalled calamity and ignorance that nursed it. The Chorus's sense of illicit knowledge and Faustus's bland anti-intellectualism both feel like poor excuses for failure. It could just as easily be argued, and more plausibly, that ignorance is the real cause of the don's downfall; and, equally, that the path to disaster has been mapped not by treacherous enlightenment but by dangerous recklessness. The contract that Faustus signs is a contract for pleasure not a contract for knowledge. The terms of the agreement, as Faustus carelessly pens them, can funnel him in no other direction. This fact he recognizes himself in the final act as his life on earth teeters near its end: "For vain pleasure of four-and-twenty years hath Faustus lost eternal joy and felicity. I writ them a bill with mine own blood" (5.2.40–42).

A few moments earlier, when Faustus was thinking of reneging on his contract, Mephistopheles had threatened to tear him apart. Faustus had volunteered immediately to reaffirm his deal with the devil, signing in blood once again (5.1.70–74). When he had initially signed in 2.1, his first questions had focused on the search for knowledge. Now, as the close of life approaches in Act 5, he has reconciled himself to the fact that only pleasure will come from his contract with the devil. His first question after this second signing turns not to knowledge, as was the case after the original signing, but to the pleasures of the body:

> One thing, good servant, let me crave of thee
> To glut the longing of my heart's desire,
> That I might have unto my paramour,
> That heavenly Helen which I saw of late . . .
>   (5.1.80–83)

Certainly, the encounter with Helen brings to a dramatic focus some of the intellectual questions of the play. Has the eminent scholar now turned to profligate debauchee, or is this how Faustus has always been?

Does the prospect of imminent death mediate in favor of the pleasures of the body rather than the discipline of the mind?

Or, more tellingly, has Faustus, after all the obfuscation and ambiguity of the preceding years, finally understood that knowledge will never flow from the impoverished terms he drafted in his own blood? If there is any truth in this last speculation, then his search for solace in the sensual entertainment of the temporal becomes understandable. It is not so much that this has become his refuge of choice—but, rather, that it has become his only refuge. Marlowe's Chorus, and Faustus himself, may reject the extension of knowledge, or even knowledge itself, but the emblematic imprints that shadow the Fortuna/Sapientia dichotomy suggest a more radical possibility—not that knowledge damned Faustus but that the failure to achieve knowledge rendered his daring experiment vacuous. To lose your soul for ignorance and vain pleasure is a waste indeed; but to lose your soul for limitless knowledge and a glimpse of divinity may have been construed as less wasteful.

* * *

The play concludes on a note of disarming and, I submit, unbelievable affirmation. In its final nine lines, the play never sounded more like an emblem book:

> CHORUS: Cut is the branch that might have
> grown full straight,
> And burnèd is Apollo's laurel bough,
> That sometime grew within this learnèd man.
> Faustus is gone. Regard his hellish fall,
> Whose fiendful fortune may exhort the wise,
> Only to wonder at unlawful things,
> Whose deepness doth entice such forward wits,
> To practise more than heavenly power permits.
>   ("The Epilogue" 1–8)

It is a statement riddled with all the purpled prose and stock literary devices of the emblem books—from the overblown pathos of "Cut is the branch" to the appeal to Apollo's burnèd bough (Apollo is nowhere else mentioned in the play), from the alliterations of "Faustus," "fall," "fiendful fortune," and "practise," "power permits" to the solemn exhortation to "Regard his hellish fall." This is the very stuff of Alciati and Whitney and Wither, clamoring to proffer sound advice and dire warning.

There was no wit more forward than Marlowe. His own life pressed its possibilities beyond the edge of decorum and legality. Most likely a spy in his university years, Marlowe was imprisoned in 1589 for brawling in the street (resulting in a man's death), arrested for counterfeiting coins in the Netherlands in 1592, bound over to keep the peace in the same year, and charged with heresy in 1593. The Coroner's report on his death, discovered by the scholar Leslie Hotson in 1925, states clearly that it was Marlowe who attacked Ingram Frizer with Frizer's knife, the knife turning on Marlowe during the struggle and stabbing him fatally above the right eye. Can such a man as this, full of the wild color and verve of life, really be asking us in *Doctor Faustus* to stay within the confines of conventional wisdom? It seems to me more likely that Marlowe is encouraging us to step closer to the edge of the great moral abyss and ask ourselves some searching questions. What is worth dying for? What is worth losing one's soul for? He dares not to answer such queries himself but in presenting for us the spectacle of Faustus's failure he implicitly invites us to consider what exactly may have constituted success.

Notes

[1] William M. Hamlin, in "'Swolne with cunning of a selfe conceit': Marlowe's Faustus and Self-Conception," has traced Faustus's preoccupation with excess and "appetite" in Act 5 to an early reference in the first act of the play. He develops this argument in "Casting Doubt in Marlowe's *Doctor Faustus*," where he asks "For what character in English Renaissance drama better exemplifies desire and appetitiveness than Faustus? What

character more thoroughly banishes the world in order to replace it with the solipsistic trappings of his fantasy . . . ?" (262).

Conclusion

All periods of history can claim something special for themselves but looking back with hindsight on the age of Marlowe there is much that commends itself as truly remarkable. Militarism, politics, religion, governance, arts, sciences, technology, commerce, empire—all of these nucleated in the reign of Elizabeth to bring forth in many instances an extraordinary harvest of progress and achievement. In drama, the more formalized modes of scripting and performance gave way to a new vibrancy that, in a few decades, saw the development of degrees of invention beyond the ken of any who had lived in generations before. Theater, once the domain of innyards and churches, burst out into an autonomous, self-validating art, affirming itself as popular, professional entertainment in purpose built structures like the Theatre (1576), the Curtain (1577), the Rose (1587), the Swan (1595), the Globe (1599), and the Fortune (1600). Such theaters were equipped with properties and technologies and possibilities beyond anything that had been seen before. To this extraordinary crucible came playwrights—among them John Heywood, Thomas Norton, Thomas Sackville, Robert Greene, Thomas Kyd, John Lyly, Christopher Marlowe, William Shakespeare, and George Peele—who had the skill and the imagination to turn space into performance, and to pen plays that have endured the tests of time and change.

On the face of it, Marlowe was in several ways dissimilar to his peers. Though he was well known and, apparently, liked, he was nonetheless different. Though from humble origins, he was university educated and while this wasn't a unique credential amongst Elizabethan playwrights it was certainly unusual for those who basked in the higher echelons of Elizabethan dramatic reputation. It's tempting to think that this is testimony of Marlowe's remarkable ability to communicate with common people in a language and through devices they could understand. All of the great playwrights of the age had this facility—they weren't simply gifted writers, they were immensely popular as well—but you might just have thought someone of Marlowe's highly educated background would have set his sights beyond the realm of mass entertainment. Not so. His knowledge of and evident relish for popular culture and character is reflected widely in his canon, not only in the portraiture of ordinary people like Dido's Nurse and the ostlers of *Doctor Faustus* but also in the array of popular emblems and icons that sparkle across the surface of his plays and whose light penetrates to the very depths of textual meaning. Marlowe's use of these devices, his manipulation and adjustment of their meanings to suit his dramatic purposes, is unrivalled amongst his peers. Compared to a play like *Edward II*, Shakespeare's use of iconographic and emblematic imagery in the *Henry VI* plays and *King John* is stodgy and inconsistent. It is only in *Richard II*, *Henry IV*, and *Henry V* that Shakespeare's art begins to challenge the work of his rival, and by that time Marlowe had been long dead.

Marlowe was also openly gay and while some of his contemporary dramatists may well have shared his sexuality, few of them were prepared to admit to it publicly. This openness about his sexuality belied the covertness of other aspects of his life. It's very likely he was a spy, and that he traveled to France particularly for this purpose. The award of his master's degree at Cambridge, in some doubt because of his absence from college, was justified and excused by the university authorities after the Privy Council intervened by letter on 29 June 1587:

> Whereas it was reported that Christopher Morley
> [*sic*] was determined to have gone beyond the seas to
> Reames and there to remaine, Their Lordships
> thought good to certefie that he had no such intent,
> but that in all his accions he had behaved him selfe
> orderlie and discreetlie wherebie he had done her
> Majestie good service, & deserved to be rewarded for
> his fathfull dealinge: Their Lordships request that
> the rumor thereof should be allaied by all possible
> meanes, and that he should be furthered in the
> degree he was to take this next Commencement:
> Because it was not her Majesties pleasure that anie
> one emploied as he had been in matters touching the
> benefitt of his Countrie should be defamed by those
> that are ignorant in th'affaires he went about.
>
> (*Privy Council Registers* PC2/14/381)

How, exactly, he had done "her Majestie good service" is unclear but it must have been an important matter of state, for the letter was signed by the Lord Archbishop, the Lord Chancellor, and the Lord Chamberlain, and no doubt was written at the behest of the queen for whom the Privy Council acted as an advisory body—a formidable array of authority. If it was spying, as most commentators now believe, then it is quite extraordinary that someone in his early twenties could have been entrusted with the daunting responsibility of espionage. What contacts and maneuverings had led to this mission we shall likely never know but something had marked Marlowe as special, as someone who had the guile and subtlety to undertake an act of the most dangerous subterfuge. It may perhaps also shed some light on the slippery qualities of his writing. So often in his theater the surface topography of meaning runs contrary to the finer nuances of the text. The devil is in the details, so to speak, and Marlowe's devils are everywhere. But this apparently natural disposition for subversion, especially political subversion, was a double-edged sword. It may explain the faceted meanings of his plays but it also points accusingly to the mystery of his death at the hands of Ingram Frizer in May 1593.

Marlowe, of course, didn't know he was going to die on that fateful night in Deptford and it is curious that we now speak of his earlier and later plays as if his canon arched over decades rather than the paltry handful of years it actually spanned. All of these plays rightfully should be considered works of his early career and yet we see such a remarkable transition from *Dido, Queen of Carthage* to *Doctor Faustus* that it is difficult to compass both as part of the same creative spur. How might Marlowe's career have evolved had he lived? That question stands as the saddest and most insoluble of all Marlovian reveries. But what we do know is that in this early, and only, phase of his career, Marlowe was constantly experimenting. Even in *Doctor Faustus* he is experimenting with ideas and images—adjusting, manipulating, inverting, subverting, maneuvering. That is exactly what we would expect from a dramatist in his early career and Marlowe doesn't disappoint us.

His deathly experiments stand as one of the most engaging aspects of his work. Death is visited upon the plays in all its gory and glorious guises. He is the soldier mower, the gentle carer, the stalking predator, the devilish ravager, the savior, the bearer of truth, the pillager of life and glory and honor. Death provides a gateway and a yardstick for measuring the quality and worth of mortal existence. It is an opportunity for an individual to confront and bring a kind of closure to the ignominy of the world. In *Dido, Queen of Carthage* the queen and her would-be lover Iarbas commit themselves through suicide to a contemptuous judgment of life and its worth. We see something similar in *Tamburlaine, Part Two* where Olympia and others prefer death to life under the sway of Tamburlaine. Death stands also as the challenge, the measure of heroic nerve, for characters to test the myths they have created around themselves and to weigh words and actions against history. In *Edward II*,

Young Mortimer and Edward both pronounce death-defying mythologies of heroism and both fall at the hurdle of their own myth-making. Death is also the measure of less heroic ambitions. The Guise, the would-be death dealer of *The Massacre at Paris*, falls short of his macabre ideal. Barabas, the aspiring Machevill of *The Jew of Malta* and perpetrator of the play's most heinous evils, boils defiantly in a cauldron for his deeds. And Faustus, pursuer of forbidden truths, must endure dismemberment by devils. All of these aspects of death, so powerfully captured in the fury and silence of Marlowe's stage, had their roots in the popular culture of Elizabethan England, a culture that would have been understood by almost everyone who entered the theaters of Marlowe's days and watched his plays.

Not everyone, though, would have grasped the deepest resonances of death in these plays. Marlowe's aptitude for subversion drew him into dangerous areas of political and religious commentary, areas where the greatest circumspection and caution were required. In *Dido, Queen of Carthage*, for example, he knew well enough that his own relatively compassionate queen, Elizabeth I, had meted out uncommonly barbarous punishments to those who had dared to question her liaison with François, Duke of Anjou. Yet, in theatricalizing a story that allowed him to draw parallels between a love struck queen and national imperatives, he dares to tread that fine line between opinion and treason. Again, in the *Tamburlaine* plays he places his drama at the center of debates about England's ambitions for empire, audaciously suggesting, in an age where such thoughts were not generally current, that someone who has a different skin color or worships a different God is as much a part of common humanity as those who walk down Elizabethan streets or sit in the stalls of the Rose Theatre. *The Massacre at Paris* provides Marlowe with a more oblique canvas to paint disturbing images of people and ideas that somehow have been able to circumvent the normative standards of civilization. The shadowy world of Elizabethan politics in post-Armada London, corrupted and convoluted by its own self-feeding power and nascent ambitions, is subjected to a scrutiny of motive and accountability that outside the medium of the theater might have cost Marlowe his liberty or even his life. In *The Jew of Malta* Marlowe turns his ironic circumspection to religion, reviling the acts of the wicked Jew and scorning the officers of Catholicism—and then, with an emblematic guile breathtaking in its impudence, sniping at the feigned piety and self-congratulating hypocrisy of those who set themselves as the religious and moral arbiters of their fellow mortals.

There are other plays that seem to speak more intimately about the nature of the man, Marlowe, himself. Had he not been gay would Marlowe's interests have drifted towards the writing of *Edward II*? Likely not. And yet the play is in no sense an advocacy for gay rights or tolerance. There is little hint of sympathy for Gaveston and only measured compassion for the king, despite the horrific nature of his death. The final moments certainly welcome the advent of the great Edward III but everything before it has studied the abject failures of individuals in their efforts to validate the myths out of which and within which they seek to live their lives. The contempt of the nobility for the king and his consort is repeatedly framed in terms of their liaison, as if their sexual orientation itself lies at the root of "the problem." Marlowe could have felt anger at this, could have used his unrivalled power of word and action to rail against their narrowness and bigotry but instead he tempers his wrath in order to reach for a higher, more measured statement about human existence. Any social or political space that a person presumes to inhabit, be it as king or courtesan, nobleman or soldier, leaves itself open to the prospect of scrutiny and the possibility of failure. There is, indeed, a problem in *Edward II*. The king is not fit to occupy his role, not fit to rule, and it leads to terrible personal tragedy. It has nothing to do with his being homosexual, just as the failure of so many others has nothing to do with their being heterosexual. The play is about what people can and cannot do, about what they are and what they are not.

Doctor Faustus, the last and greatest achievement of young Christopher Marlowe's life, embraces so many of those glorious qualities and moments that articulated the young dramatist's own life and thinking—

university days, travel, the yearning for knowledge, the friendships in an academic milieu, the idealistic quest for the betterment of humankind. There is here, too, an eerie sense of isolation. Few characters in plays of Marlowe's period spend as much time as Faustus does with us, his audience. He is often alone on stage with his thoughts, and in places with which he is not familiar—a stranger and a wanderer who in the privacy of his mind seeks that which is forbidden. Could this perhaps have been Marlowe himself? How much more sympathy do we feel for Faustus than we do for Barabas or Tamburlaine or even Dido and Edward II? Faustus, like Eve in the Garden of Eden, has reached for knowledge that lies beyond his rightful claim. It is a fearful crime and he is punished fearfully but in his dream and in his failure perhaps we recognize the fallible spark of our own humanity.

Bibliography

Alciati, Andrea. *Andreas Alciatus. 1: The Latin Emblems, Indexes and Lists.* Ed. Peter M. Daly. Toronto: U of Toronto P, 1988.

———. *Emblemata.* Padua: Tozzi, 1621.

———. *Emblematum Libellus.* Paris: Christian Wechel, 1534.

———. *Emblematum Liber.* Augsburg: Heinrich Steyner, 1531.

Archer, John Michael. *Sovereignty and Intelligence: Spying and Court Culture in the English Renaissance.* Stanford: Stanford UP, 1993.

Ariès, Phillipe. *Western Attitudes toward Death: From the Middle Ages to the Present.* Trans. Patricia M. Ranum. Baltimore: Johns Hopkins UP, 1974.

Baines, Richard. The Baines Note, BL Harley MS.6848 ff.185–86.

Banerjee, Pompa. "I, Mephastophilis: Self, Other, and Demonic Parody in Marlowe's *Doctor Faustus.*" *Christianity and Literature* 42.2 (1993): 221–41.

Bartels, Emily C. *Spectacles of Strangeness: Imperialism, Alienation, and Marlowe.* Philadelphia: U of Pennsylvania P, 2003.

Bartsch, Adam. *Le Peintre Graveur.* Leipzig: J. A. Barth, 1866.

Batman, Stephen. *The Golden Booke of the Leaden Goddes.* 1577. Rpt. New York and London: Garland, 1976.

Bear, Elizabeth. *Hell and Earth: A Novel of the Promethean Age*. London: Roc, 2008.

Beaumont, Francis. *The Knight of the Burning Pestle*. Ed. Andrew Gurr. Berkeley: U of California P, 1966.

Bennett, H. S., ed. The Jew of Malta *and* The Massacre at Paris, *by Christopher Marlowe*. 1931. Rpt. New York: Gordian P, 1966.

Bennett, Josephine Waters. "Britain among The Fortunate Isles," *Studies in Philology*, 53 (1956): 114–40.

Bevington, David M. and Eric Rasmussen, eds. *Doctor Faustus*. Manchester: Manchester UP, 1993.

Bevington, David M. and James Shapiro. "'What are Kings, When regiment is Gone?' The Decay of Ceremony in *Edward II*." "*A Poet and a Filthy Play-Maker": New Essays on Christopher Marlowe*. Ed. Kenneth Friedenreich, Roma Gill, and Constance B. Kuriyama. New York: AMS, 1988. 263–78.

Bingham, Captain. Prefatory Poem in George Peckham's *A Trve Report, Of the late discoueries, and possession, taken in the right of the Crowne of Englande, of the New-found Landes*. Longon: John Hinde, 1583.

Birringer, Johannes H. "Marlowe's Violent Stage: Mirrors of Honor in *Tamburlaine*." *ELH* 51 (1984): 219–39.

Boas, F. S. *Marlowe: A Biographical and Critical Study*. Oxford: Oxford UP, 1953.

Boccaccio, Giovanni. *The Fall of Princes. A Treatise excellent and compendious, shewing the falls of sundry most notable Princes and Princesses with other nobles*. Trans. John Lydgate. London: Richard Tottel, 1554.

Bocchi, Achille. *Symbolicarum Quaestionum, De vniuerso genere, quas serio ludebat, Libri Qvinqve*. 1555. Bononiae: apud Societatem Typographiae Bononiensis, 1574.

Bossewell, John. *Workes of armorie, deuyded into three bookes, entituled, the Concordes of armorie, the Armorie of honor, and of Coates and creastes*. London: Richardi Totelli, 1572.

Bowers, Rick. "*The Massacre at Paris*: Marlowe's Messy Consensus Narrative." *Marlowe, History, and Sexuality: New Critical Essays on*

Christopher Marlowe. Ed. Paul Whitfield White. New York: AMS, 1998. 131–41.

Briggs, Julia. "Marlowe's *Massacre at Paris*: A Reconsideration." *Review of English Studies: A Quarterly Journal of English Literature and the English Language* 34 (1983): 257–78.

Brown, Georgia. *Redefining Elizabethan Literature*. Cambridge: Cambridge UP, 2005.

Brown, William J. "Marlowe's Debasement of Bajazet: Foxe's *Actes and Monuments* and *Tamburlaine, Part 1.*" *Renaissance Quarterly* 24 (1971): 38–48.

Bullough, Geoffrey. *Narrative and Dramatic Sources of Shakespeare*, Vol. III. London: Routledge & Kegan Paul, 1960.

Burgess, Anthony. *A Dead Man in Deptford*. London: Hutchinson, 1993.

Burnett, Mark Thornton, ed. *The Complete Plays* by Christopher Marlowe. London: Everyman, J. M. Dent, 1999.

———. "Tamburlaine and the Body." *Criticism: A Quarterly for Literature and the Arts* 33 (1991): 31–47.

Burton, Jonathan. "Anglo-Ottoman Relations and the Image of the Turk in *Tamburlaine*." *Journal of Medieval and Early Modern Studies* 30 (2000): 125–56.

Calendrier des Bergers. Icy est le compost et kalendrier des Bergiers Nouuellement refait et austrement compose que nestoit parauant. Paris: Guy Marchant and Antoine Vérard, 1493.

Callaghan, Dympna. "The Terms of Gender: 'Gay' and 'Feminist' *Edward II.*" *Feminist Readings of Early Modern Culture: Emerging Subjects*. Eds. Valerie Traub, M. Lindsay Kaplan, and Dympna Callaghan. Cambridge: Cambridge UP, 1996. 275–301.

Campion, Thomas. *Two Books of Agnes*. A. H. Bullen, ed. London: A. H. Bullen, 1903.

Carroll, Tim. Director of *Dido, Queen of Carthage*. London: Shakespeare's Globe Theatre, June 2003.

Cartari, Vincenzo. *Le imagini de i dei de gli antichi*. Venice: Francesco Marcolini, 1556.

Chamberlain, Arthur B. *Hans Holbein The Younger*. Vol. 1. London: George Allen, 1913.

Charney, Maurice. "Marlowe's *Edward II* as Model for Shakespeare's *Richard II*." *Research Opportunities in the Renaissance Drama* 33 (1994): 31–41.

Chaucer, Geoffrey. *The Canterbury Tales*. Ed. Jill Mann. London: Penguin Classics, 2005.

Chronycles of Englande. St. Albans, Hertfordshire: William Caxton, 1483.

Clark, James M. *The Dance of Death by Hans Holbein*. London: Phaidon, 1947.

———. *The Dance of Death in the Middle Ages and the Renaissance*. Glasgow: Jackson, 1950.

Cole, Douglas. *Suffering and Evil in the Plays of Christopher Marlowe*. Princeton: Princeton UP, 1962.

Combe, Thomas, trans. *The Theater of Fine Devices Containing an Hundred Morall Emblems*, by Guillaume de la Perrière. 1593. London: R. Field, 1614.

Cook, Judith. *The Slicing Edge of Death*. London: Simon & Schuster, 1993.

Cooper, Geoffrey and Christopher Wortham, eds. *Everyman*. Nedlands: U of Western Australia P, 1980.

Corrozet, Gilles. *Hecatongraphie. C'est à dire les descriptions de cent figures & hystoires*. Paris: Denys Ianot, 1543.

Coustau, Pierre. *Le Pegme de Pierre Coustau*. Lyons: Barthelemy Molin, 1560.

Cox, John D. "Devils and Power in Marlowe and Shakespeare." *Yearbook of English Studies* 23 (1993): 46–64.

Daly, Peter M., ed. *Andreas Alciatus. 1: The Latin Emblems, Indexes and Lists*. Toronto: U of Toronto P, 1988.

Daniel, Samuel. *The Civile Wares betweene the Howses of Lancaster and Yorke*. 1595. London: Simon Waterson, 1609.

Daye, John, ed. *Seven Sermons made vpon the Lordes Prayer by Hugh Latimer*. London: John Daye, 1571.

Daza, Bernardino. *Emblemas*. Lyon: Bonhomme, 1549.

Deats, Sarah Munson. "Myth and Metamorphosis in Marlowe's *Edward II.*" *Texas Studies in Literature and Language: A Journal of the Humanities* 22 (1980): 304–21.

———. *Sex, Gender, and Desire in the Plays of Christopher Marlowe.* Newark: U of Delaware P, 1997.

de Bovelles, Charles. *Liber De Sapeinte.* Paris: 1510.

de Bry, Theodore. *Emblemata nobilitate et vulgo scitu digna.* Frankfurt am Main: [Theodore de Bry], 1592.

de la Perrière, Guillaume. *Le Theatre des bons engins auquel sont contenuz cent Emblemes moraulx.* Paris, Denis Janot, 1544.

DeMaria, Robert. *To Be a King: A Novel About Christopher Marlowe.* New York: Amerion, 1999.

de Montenay, Georgette. *Emblematvm Christianorvm Centvria.* 1571. Tigvri [Zurich]: 1584.

DiGangi, Mario. "Marlowe, Queer Studies, and Renaissance Homo-eroticism." *Marlowe, History, and Sexuality: New Critical Essays on Christopher Marlowe.* Ed. Paul Whitfield White. New York: AMS, 1998. 195–212.

Donne, John. *The Complete Poetry and Selected Prose of John Donne.* Ed. Charles M. Coffin. New York: Modern Library, 1994.

Douce, Francis. *Dissertation on the Various Designs of the Dance of Death.* London: 1833.

Douglas, Gavin, trans. *Virgil's Aeneid.* Ed. David F. C. Coldwell. 4 vols. Edinburgh: Blackwood for the Scottish Text Society, 1957–64.

Du Bartas, Guillaume de Salluste. *Du Bartas. His Diuine Weekes and Workes with A Compleate Collectiō of all the other most delight-full Workes.* Trans. Joshua Sylvester. London: 1605.

Emsley, Sarah. "'I Cannot Love, to Be an Emperess': Women and Honour in *Tamburlaine.*" *Dalhousie Review* 80 (2000): 169–86.

Evans, G. Blakemore, et al., eds. *The Riverside Shakespeare.* Boston: Houghton Mifflin, 1997.

Everyman. Eds. Geoffrey Cooper and Christopher Wortham. Nedlands. U of Western Australia P, 1980.

Feola, Maryann. "A Poniard's Point of Satire in Marlowe's *The Massacre at Paris*." *English Language Notes* 35.4 (June 1998): 6–12.

Foxe, John. *Actes and Monuments of these latter and perillous dayes, touching matters of the Church, wherein ar[e] comprehended and described the great persecutions & horrible troubles, that haue bene wrought and practised by the Romishe Prelates, speciallye in this Realme of England and Scotlande, from the yeare of our Lorde a thousande, vnto the tyme nowe present.* London: John Daye, 1563.

Freeman, Rosemary. *English Emblem Books*. 1948. London: Chatto and Windus, 1967.

Freitag, Arnold. *Mythologia ethica, hoc est, Moralis philosophiae per fabulas brutis attributas ... viridarium ... / artificiosiss[im]is nobilissimorum sculptoru[m] iconib[us] ab Arnoldo Freitagio Embricensi, latine explicatis, [ae]ri incisum*. Antwerp: Christopher Plantin, 1579.

Frieda, Leonie. *Catherine de Medici*. London: Phoenix, 2005.

Gamel, Mary-Kay. "The Triumph of Cupid: Marlowe's *Dido, Queen of Carthage*." *American Journal of Philology* 126 (2005): 613–22.

Gascoigne, George. "The Spanish Fury." London: 1576.

Gatti, Hilary. *The Renaissance Drama of Knowledge: Giordano Bruno in England*. London: Routledge, 1989.

Geoffrey of Monmouth. *Historia Britonum*. Ed. J. A. Giles. London: D. Nutt, 1844.

Gerould, G. H. "King Arthur and Politics." *Speculum* 2 (1927): 33–51.

Gertsman, Elina, "Pleyinge and Peyntynge: Performing the Dance of Death." *Studies in Iconography* 27 (2006): 1–43.

Glenn, John R. "The Martyrdom of Ramus in Marlowe's *The Massacre at Paris*." *Papers on Language and Literature: A Journal for Scholars and Critics of Languages and Literature* 9 (1973): 365–79.

Godman, Maureen. "Stow's *Summarie*: Source for Marlowe's *Edward II*." *Notes and Queries* new series 40.2 (June 1993): 160–63.

Godshalk, William Leigh. "Marlowe's *Dido, Queen of Carthage*." *ELH* 38.1 (1971): 1–18.

Green, Henry. *Shakespeare and the Emblem Writers*. London: Trübner, 1870.

Greenblatt, Stephen. *Renaissance Self-Fashioning: From More to Shakespeare.* Chicago: U of Chicago P, 1980.

Greene, Robert. *The Spanish Masquerado.* London: 1589.

Greg, W. W., ed. *The Massacre at Paris*, by Christopher Marlowe. Malone Society Reprint. Oxford: Oxford UP, 1928.

Hamlin, William M. "Casting Doubt in Marlowe's *Doctor Faustus.*" *Studies in English Literature* 41.2 (2001): 257–75.

———. "'Swolne with cunning of a selfe conceit': Marlowe's Faustus and Self-Conception." *English Language Notes* 34.2 (1996): 7–13.

Hammill, Graham L. *Sexuality and Form: Caravaggio, Marlowe, and Bacon.* Chicago: U of Chicago P, 2000.

Hendricks, Margo. "Managing the Barbarian: The Tragedy of *Dido, Queen of Carthage.*" *Renaissance Drama* 2 (1992): 165–88.

Henkel, Arthur and Albrecht Schöne, eds. *Emblemata: Handbuch zur Sinnbildkunst des XVI. und XVII. Jahrhunderts.* Stuttgart: J. B. Metzlersche Verlagsbuchhandlung, 1967.

Herbert, Sir Thomas. *A relation of some yeares travaile begunne anno 1626, into Afrique and the greater Asia.* 1634. London: 1638.

Herbrüggen, Hubertus Schulte. "*La Danse macabre*, the English Dance of Death, and William Drury's *Mors Comoedia.*" *Acta Conventus Neo-Latini Torontonensis.* Eds. Alexander Dalzell and Charles Fantazzi. Binghampton, New York: Medieval and Renaissance Texts and Studies, 1991.

Hiscock, Andrew. "Enclosing 'Infinite Riches in a Little Room': The Question of Cultural Marginality in Marlowe's *The Jew of Malta.*" *Forum for Modern Languages Studies* 35.1 (1999): 1–22.

Holbein, Hans. *Icones Historiarvm Veteris Testamenti.* Lyon: Jean and François Frellon, 1547.

———. *Imagines Mortis. His acceserunt, Epigrammata, e Gallico idiomate a Georgio Aemylio in Latinum translate.* Lyon: Jean and François Frellon, 1545.

———. *Les Simulachres & Historiees faces de la Mort, avtant elegammet pourtraictes, que artificiellement imagines.* Lyon: Trechsel, 1538.

Holinshed, Raphael. *The first (laste) volume of the chronicles of England, Scotlande, and Ireland*. 1577. London: 1807–08.

———. *Holinshed's Chronicle*. Eds. Allardyce Nicoll and Josephine Nicoll. London: Dent, 1965.

Homer, *The Odyssey*. Ed. D. C. H. Rieu. Trans. E. V. Rieu. Intro. Peter Jones. London: Penguin Classics, 2010.

Hopkins, Lisa. *Christopher Marlowe: A Literary Life*. New York: St. Martin's, 2000.

Hunger, Wolfgang. *Emblemata*. Paris: Christian Wechel, 1542.

Hunter, G. K. "The Theology of Marlowe's *The Jew of Malta*." *Journal of the Warburg and Courtauld Institute* 27 (1964): 211–40.

Jackson, MacDonald P. "Shakespeare and the Quarrel Scene in Arden of Faversham." *Shakespeare Quarterly* 57.3 (2006): 249–93.

James, L. L. "The Dramatic Effects of the Play-Within-a-Play in Shakespeare's *Hamlet* and Marlowe's *Dr. Faustus*." *Litteraria Pragensia: Studies in Literature and Culture* 5.9 (1995): 17–31.

Jourdan, Silvester. "The Epistle Dedicatorie." *A Plaine Description of the Barmvdas, now called Sommer Ilands*. London: 1613.

Kay, Dennis. "Marlowe, Edward II, and the Cult of Elizabeth." *Early Modern Literary Studies: A Journal of Sixteenth- and Seventeenth-Century English Literature* 3.2 (1997): 30 paragraphs.

Kelly, William B. "Mapping Subjects in Marlowe's Edward II." *South Atlantic Review* (Winter 1998) 63: 1–19.

Kermode, Lloyd Edward. "'Marlowe's Second City': The Jew as Critic at the Rose in 1592." *Studies in English Literature, 1500–1900* 35.2 (Spring 1995): 215–29.

Kiefer, Frederick. "The Conflation of Fortuna and Occasio in Renaissance Thought and Iconography." *Journal of Medieval and Renaissance Studies* 9 (1979): 1–27.

Kirk, Andrew M. "Marlowe and the Discovered Face of French History." *Studies in English Literature 1500–1900* 35.2 (Spring 1995): 193–213.

Knight, W. F. Jackson, trans. *The Aeneid by Virgil*. Harmondsworth: Penguin, 1972.

Knoblochtzer, Henri. *Doten dantz mit figuren, clage und antwort schon von allen staten der werlt*. Heidelberg: ca. 1486.

Kyd, Thomas. *The Spanish Tragedy*. Ed. J. R. Mulryne. *Elizabethan and Jacobean Tragedies: A New Mermaid Anthology*. Introd. by Brian Gibbons. Tonbridge, Kent: Ernest Benn, 1984.

Larkin. Philip. *The Whitsun Weddings*. London: Faber & Faber, 1964.

Laroque, François. "Ovidian V(o)ices in Marlowe and Shakespeare: The Actaeon Variations." *Shakespeare's Ovid: The Metamorphoses in the Plays and Poems*. Ed. A. B. Taylor. Cambridge: Cambridge UP, 2000. 165–77.

Latimer, Hugh. *Seven Sermons made vpon the Lordes Prayer*. Ed. John Daye. London: John Daye, 1571.

Lefèvre, Jehan. *Emblèmes*. Paris: Wechel, 1536.

Leigh, Gerard. *The Accedence of Armorie*. 1562. London: R. Tottel, 1591.

Lerner, Robert E., Standish Meacham, and Edward McNall Burns. *Western Civilizations: Their History and Their Culture*. New York: W. W. Norton, 1993.

Levin, Carol. "John Foxe and the Responsibilities of Queenship." *Women in the Middle Ages and the Renaissance: Literary and Historical Perspectives*. Ed. Mary Beth Rose. Syracuse: Syracuse UP, 1986. 13–33.

Linche, Richard. *The Fovntaine of Ancient Fiction*. 1599. New York: Garland, 1976.

Lodge, Thomas. *The Wounds of Civil War*. Ed. Joseph W. Houppert. London: Edward Arnold, 1969.

Lydgate, John, trans. *The Fall of Princes. A Treatise excellent and compendious, shewing the falls of sundry most notable Princes and Princesses with other nobles by Giovanni Boccaccio*. London: Richard Tottel, 1554.

MacCaffrey, Wallace T. *Queen Elizabeth and the Making of Policy, 1572–88*. Princeton: Princeton UP, 1981.

Machiavelli, Niccolo. *The Prince and The Discourses*. New York: Random House, 1940.

MacKenzie, Clayton G. "Paradise and Paradise Lost in *Richard II.*" *Shakespeare Quarterly* 37 (1986): 318–39.

Mâle, Emile. *L'Art Religieux de la fin du Moyen Âge en France.* Paris: Librairie Armand Colin, 1908.

Marchant, Guy. *La danse macabre.* Paris: 1485.

Marlowe, Christopher. *The Complete Plays.* Ed. Mark Thornton Burnett. London: Everyman, J. M. Dent, 1999.

———. *Doctor Faustus.* Eds. David M. Bevington and Eric Rasmussen. Manchester: Manchester UP, 1993.

Marquale, Giovanni. *Imprese.* Lyon: Bonhomme, 1551.

Marston, John. *The Malcontent and Other Plays.* Ed. Keith Sturgess. Oxford: Oxford UP, 1997.

McAdam, Ian. "Edward II and the Illusion of Integrity." *Studies in Philology* 92 (1995): 203–29.

McKerrow, Ronald, ed. *The Works of Thomas Nashe.* Vol. 4. London: Bullen, 1904–1910.

McNatt, Glenn. "Cambodians Stare at Us, and Ask Why They Must Die," *The Baltimore Sun.* The Baltimore Sun. 27 July 1997. Web.

Merriam, Thomas. "Marlowe and Nashe in *Dido, Queen of Carthage.*" *Notes and Queries* new series 47.4 (December 2000): 425–28.

Moore, Roger E. "The Spirit and the Letter: Marlowe's *Tamburlaine* and Elizabethan Religious Radicalism." *Studies in Philology* 99 (2002): 123–51

Morice, James. *A briefe treatise of Oathes exacted by Ordinaries and Ecclesiasticall Iudges, to answere generallie to such Articles or Interrogatories, as pleaseth them to propound. And of their forced and constrained Oathes ex officio, wherein is proued that the same are vnlawfull.* London: Richard Schilders, 1590.

Nicholl, Charles. *The Reckoning: The Murder of Christopher Marlowe.* London: Vintage, 2002.

Normand, Lawrence. "'What Passions Call You These?' Edward II and James VI." *Christopher Marlowe and English Renaissance Culture.* Eds.

Darryll Grantley and Peter Roberts. Aldershot, England: Scolar, 1996. 172–95.

North, Thomas, trans. *Plutarch's Lives, Englished by Sir Thomas North in Ten Volumes.* London: 1579.

Oliver, H. J., ed. Dido, Queen of Carthage *and* The Massacre at Paris. Cambridge: Harvard UP, 1968.

Oosterwijk, Sophie. "Lessons in 'hopping': The Dance of Death and the Chester Mystery Cycle." *Comparative Drama* 36 (2002/2003): 249–87.

Panofsky, Erwin. *Studies in Iconology: Humanistic Themes in the Art of the Renaissance.* New York: Harper & Row, 1972.

Paradin, Claude. *Les Devises Heroiques, de M. Claude Paradin, chanoine de Beaujeu, du Seigneur Gabriel Symeon, & autres aucteurs.* Anvers: Christopher Plantin, 1557.

Pati, Mitali R. "The Deranged Metaphor of the King's Body Politic in Marlowe's *Edward II.*" *Explorations in Renaissance Culture* 20 (1994): 157–73.

Patterson, Steven J. "Pleasure's Likeness." Diss. Temple U, 1997.

Peacham, Henry. *Minerva Britanna: Or A Garden of Heroycal Devices.* London: William Dight, 1612.

Pieters, Jürgen. "'Be silent then, for danger is in words'. The Wonders of Reading and the Duties of Criticism." *English Studies* 2 (2001): 106–14.

Plutarch. *Plutarch's Lives of the Noble Grecians and Romans Englished by Sir Thomas North.* Trans. Sir Thomas North. Vol. 6. 1579. London: David Nutt, 1896.

Poole, Kristen Elizabeth. "Garbled Martyrdom in Christopher Marlowe's *The Massacre at Paris.*" *Comparative Drama* 32.1 (Spring 1998): 1–25.

Privy Council Registers PC2/14/381. (29 June 1587.) [Letter to the University of Cambridge from the Privy Council.]

Raleigh, Walter. *Selections from His Writings.* Oxford: Clarendon, 1917.

Rastell, John. *The Pastyme of the People The Chronycles of dyuers realmys and most specyally of the realme of England.* London: 1529.

Record, Robert. *The Castle of Knowledge*. London: R. Wolfe, 1556.

Richards, Susan. "Marlowe's *Tamburlaine II*: A Drama of Death." *Modern Language Quarterly* 26 (1965): 375–87.

Riggs, David. *The World of Christopher Marlowe*. London: Faber & Faber, 2005.

Roberts, Penny. "Marlowe's *Massacre at Paris*: A Historical Perspective." *Renaissance Studies: Journal of the Society for Renaissance Studies* 9.4 (December 1995): 430–41.

Rothschild, Herbert B., Jr. "The Conqueror Hero, the Besieged City, and the Development of an Elizabethan Protagonist." *South Central Review: The Journal of the South Central Modern Language Association* 3 (1986): 54–55.

Rusche, H. G. "Two Proverbial Images in Whitney's *A Choice of Emblemes* and Marlowe's *The Jew of Malta*." *Notes and Queries* new series 11.7 (July 1964): 261.

Ryan, Patrick. "Marlowe's *Edward II* and the Medieval Passion Play." *Comparative Drama* 32 (1998): 465–95.

Saviolo, Vincentio. *Vincentio Saviolo, His Practise. In two Bookes. The first intreating of the vse of the Rapier and Dagger. The second, of Honor and honorable Quarrels*. London: John Wolfe, 1595.

Schuman, Samuel. "'Occasion's bald behind': A Note on the Sources of an Emblematic Image in *The Jew of Malta*." *Modern Philology: A Journal Devoted to Research in Medieval and Modern Literature* 70 (1973): 234–35.

Shakespeare, William. *The Riverside Shakespeare*. Eds. G. Blakemore Evans, et al. Boston: Houghton Mifflin, 1997.

Shepherd, Simon. *Marlowe and the Politics of Elizabethan Theatre*. Brighton: Harvester, 1986.

Simeoni, Gabriel. *Pvrtratvres Or Emblemes of Gabriel Simeon, a Florentine. The Heroicall Devises of M. Clavdivs Paradin Canon of Beauieu, whereunto are added the Lord Gabriel Symeons and others*. Trans. P. S. London: William Kearney, 1591.

Smith, Robert A. H. "*Julius Caesar* and *The Massacre at Paris.*" *Notes and Queries* 44.4 (December 1997): 496–97.

Somerset, Anne. *Elizabeth I.* London: Phoenix, 1997.

Speed, John. *The History of Great Britaine Under the conquests of [the] Romans, Saxons, Danes and Normans.* 1572. London: John Sudbury and George Humble, 1611.

Starks, Lisa S. "'Won with thy words and conquered with thy looks': Sadism, Masochism, and the Masochistic Gaze in *1 Tamburlaine.*" *Marlowe, History, and Sexuality: New Critical Essays on Christopher Marlowe.* Ed. Paul Whitfield White. New York: AMS, 1998. 179–93.

Stocker, Thomas. "Epistle Dedicatorie." *A Tragicall Historie of the troubles and Ciuile Warres of the lowe Countries, otherwise called Flanders.* London: John Kyngston and Thomas Dawson, 1583.

Stow, John. *A Survay of London; contayning the originall, antiquity, increase, moderne estate, and description of that citie.* London: J. Wolfe, 1598.

Stump, Donald. "Marlowe's Travesty of Virgil: Dido and Elizabethan Dreams of Empire." *Comparative Drama* 34 (2000): 79–107.

Summers, Claude J. "Sex, Politics, and Self-Realization in *Edward II.*" *"A Poet and a Filthy Play-Maker": New Essays on Christopher Marlowe.* Eds. Kenneth Friedenreich, Roma Gill, and Constance B. Kuriyama. New York: AMS, 1988. 221–40.

Sutcliffe, Matthew. *The Practice, Proceedings, And Lawes of armes, described out of the doings of most valiant and expert Captaines, and confirmed both by ancient, and moderne examples, and praecedents.* London: Christopher Barker, 1593.

Sylvester, Joshua, trans. *Du Bartas. His Diuine Weekes and Workes with A Compleate Collectiō of all the other most delight-full Workes.* London: 1605.

Tate, William. "Solomon, Gender, and Empire in Marlowe's *Doctor Faustus.*" *Studies in English Literature* 37.2 (1997): 257–76.

Thomson, Sarah L. *The Secret of the Rose.* New York: Greenwillow, 2006.

Thurn, David H. "Sights of Power in *Tamburlaine.*" *English Literary Renaissance* 19 (1989): 3–21.

Van der Noot, Jan. *A Theatre for Worldlings. A theatre wherein be represented as wel the miseries and calamities that follow the voluptuous Worldlings, As also the greate joyes and pleasures which the faithfull do enjoy. An Argument both profitable and delectable, to all that sincerely love the word of God*. London: Henry Bynneman, 1569.

Virgil. *The Aeneid*. Trans. W. F. Jackson Knight. Harmondsworth: Penguin, 1972.

Webb, David C. "Damnation in *Doctor Faustus*: Theological Strip Tease and the Histrionic Hero." *Critical Survey* 11.1 (1999): 31–47.

Whelan, Peter. *The School of the Night*. London: Warner Chappell, 1992.

Whitney, Geffrey. *A Choice of Emblemes*. Leyden: Christopher Plantin, 1586.

Wilders, John. *The Lost Garden: A View of Shakespeare's English and Roman Plays*. London: Macmillan, 1978.

Williams, Deanne. "Dido, Queen of England." *ELH* 73.1 (2006): 31–60.

Wither, George. *A Collection of Emblemes, Ancient and Moderne (1635)*. Ed. Michael Bath. Aldershot, England: Scolar Press, 1989.

———. *A Collection of Emblemes, Ancient and Moderne (1635)*. Ed. Rosemary Freeman. Columbia: U of South Carolina P, 1975.

Wyrley, William. *The Trve Vse of Armorie, Shewed by Historie, and plainly proued by example*. London: J. Jackson for Gabriell Cawood, 1592.

Index

Opportunity, 43
Ovid, 5
Pallas, 58, 59, 60, 68–70
Panofsky, Erwin, 43
Paradin, Claude, 21
Paradise. *See* Eden/Paradise
Pardon Churchyard (St. Paul's Cathedral, London), 74
Paris, and Helen, 103
Pastyme of the People, The (Rastell), 53
Pati, Mitali R., 67
Peacham, Henry, 58, 59, 60, 70; "Quæ pondere maior," 58, 59
Peckham, George, 71n1
"Pedlar, The" (Holbein), 28, 30, 75–76
Peele, George, 117
Pegme de Pierre Coustau, Le (Coustau), 33
pictura/picturae, xvii, xx, xxiv, 15
"Pietas in patriam" (Whitney), 36
Pieters, Jürgen, 111
Pilgrims Way, 45
Plutarch, 91
Poole, Kristen Elizabeth, xvi, 78, 86
Pope Adrian, 100
Pope Bruno, 100
"Potentissimus affectus, amor" (Whitney), 5
Practice, Proceedings, And Lawes of armes, The (Sutcliffe), 53

Prince, The (Machiavelli), 40
Privy Council Registers, 119
Privy Council, 119
Pvrtratvres Or Emblemes (Simeoni), 46
"Quæ pondere maior" (Peacham), 58, 59
Raleigh, Sir Walter, 35
Rasmussen, Eric, xix, xxvin2
Rastell, John, 53
Record, Robert, 107, 108, 113
Redefining Elizabethan Literature (Brown), 99
Reformation, 87
Richard II (Shakespeare), xxii, 11, 34, 38n1, 52–53, 72n2, 118
Richards, Susan, 15, 35
Riggs, David, xv
Riverside Shakespeare, xxvin3
Roberts, Penny, 77
Rochester Cathedral (Kent), 44
Rome, 100
Romeo and Juliet (Shakespeare), 10–11
Rose Theatre, xvi, 117, 121
Rosslyn Church (near Edinburgh), 87
Rothschild, Herbert B., Jr., 85
Roxana, 100
Rusche, H. G., 43
Ryan, Patrick, 70
Satan, 100. *See also* Devil/devils
Saviolo, Vincentio, 21